New Daylight

Edited by Naomi Starkey

September–December 2015

New Daylight © BRF 2015

The Bible Reading Fellowship
15 The Chambers, Vineyard, Abingdon OX14 3FE
Tel: 01865 319700; Fax: 01865 319701
E-mail: enquiries@brf.org.uk; Website: www.brf.org.uk

ISBN 978 0 85746 132 2

Distributed in Australia by Mediacom Education Inc., PO Box 610, Unley, SA 5061.
Tel: 1800 811 311; Fax: 08 8297 8719;
E-mail: admin@mediacom.org.au
Available also from all good Christian bookshops in Australia.
For individual and group subscriptions in Australia:
Mrs Rosemary Morrall, PO Box W35, Wanniassa, ACT 2903.

Distributed in New Zealand by Scripture Union Wholesale, PO Box 760, Wellington
Tel: 04 385 0421; Fax: 04 384 3990; E-mail: suwholesale@clear.net.nz

Publications distributed to more than 60 countries

Acknowledgments

The New Revised Standard Version of the Bible, Anglicised Edition, copyright © 1989, 1995 by the Division of Christian Education of the National Council of the Churches of Christ in the USA. Used by permission. All rights reserved.

The Holy Bible, New International Version, Anglicised edition, copyright © 1979, 1984, 2011 by Biblica. Used by permission of Hodder & Stoughton Publishers, an Hachette UK company. All rights reserved. 'NIV' is a registered trademark of Biblica. UK trademark number 1448790.

Scripture quotations from the Good News Bible published by The Bible Societies/HarperCollins Publishers Ltd, UK © American Bible Society 1966, 1971, 1976, 1992, used with permission.

Extracts from the Authorised Version of the Bible (The King James Bible), the rights in which are vested in the Crown, are reproduced by permission of the Crown's Patentee, Cambridge University Press.

Scripture quotations taken from the Holy Bible, English Standard Version, published by HarperCollins Publishers, © 2001 Crossway Bibles, a division of Good News Publishers. Used by permission. All rights reserved.

Scripture taken from THE MESSAGE. Copyright © 1993, 1994, 1995, 1996, 2000, 2001, 2002. Used by permission of NavPress Publishing Group.

The Revised Common Lectionary is copyright © The Consultation on Common Texts, 1992 and is reproduced with permission. *The Christian Year: Calendar, Lectionary and Collects*, which includes the *Common Worship* lectionary (the Church of England's adaptations of the *Revised Common Lectionary*, published as the Principal Service lectionary) is copyright © The Central Board of Finance of the Church of England, 1995, 1997, and material from it is reproduced with permission.

Printed by Gutenberg Press, Tarxien, Malta.

Suggestions for using New Daylight

Find a regular time and place, if possible, where you can read and pray undisturbed. Before you begin, take time to be still and perhaps use the BRF prayer. Then read the Bible passage slowly (try reading it aloud if you find it over-familiar), followed by the comment. You can also use New Daylight for group study and discussion, if you prefer.

The prayer or point for reflection can be a starting point for your own meditation and prayer. Many people like to keep a journal to record their thoughts about a Bible passage and items for prayer. In New Daylight we also note the Sundays and some special festivals from the Church calendar, to keep in step with the Christian year.

New Daylight and the Bible

New Daylight contributors use a range of Bible versions, and you will find a list of the versions used opposite, on page 2. You are welcome to use your own preferred version alongside the passage printed in the notes. This can be particularly helpful if the Bible text has been abridged.

New Daylight affirms that the whole of the Bible is God's revelation to us, and we should read, reflect on and learn from every part of both Old and New Testaments. Usually the printed comment presents a straight-forward 'thought for the day', but sometimes it may also raise questions rather than simply providing answers, as we wrestle with some of the more difficult passages of Scripture.

New Daylight is also available in a deluxe edition (larger format). Visit your local Christian bookshop or contact the BRF office, who can also give details about a cassette version for the visually impaired. For a Braille edition, contact St John's Guild, Sovereign House, 12–14 Warwick Street, Coventry CV5 6ET.

Comment on New Daylight

To send feedback, you may email or write to BRF at the addresses shown opposite. If you would like your comment to be included on our website, please email connect@brf.org.uk. You can also Tweet to @brfonline, using the hashtag #brfconnect.

Writers in this issue

Steve Aisthorpe lives in Scotland with his wife and two sons. He is a Mission Development Worker for the Church of Scotland, encouraging mission and discipleship throughout the Highlands and Islands.

John Twisleton is parish priest of Horsted Keynes in West Sussex. He is the author of Using the Jesus Prayer (BRF, 2014) and broadcasts regularly on Premier Christian Radio.

Bob Mayo is a vicar in Shepherds Bush and the chaplain at QPR. He is a keen runner and ran his twelfth marathon in Bethlehem in order to bring attention to the situation in the Middle East.

Penelope Wilcock writes Christian fiction, pastoral theology and Bible study. Her books include *Spiritual Care of Dying and Bereaved People* (BRF, 2013). She blogs at http://kindredofthequietway.blogspot.co.uk.

Michael Mitton is a freelance writer, speaker and consultant and the Fresh Expressions Adviser for the Derby Diocese. He is also the NSM Priest-in-charge of St Paul's Derby and honorary Canon of Derby Cathedral. He is the author of *Travellers of the Heart* (BRF, 2013).

Naomi Starkey is a Commissioning Editor for BRF and edits and writes for New Daylight Bible reading notes. She has also written The Recovery of Love (BRF, 2012).

Rachel Boulding is Deputy Editor of the *Church Times*. Before this, she was Senior Editor at SPCK, and then Senior Liturgy Editor at Church House Publishing. She lives in Dorset with her husband and son.

Helen Julian CSF is an Anglican Franciscan sister, currently serving her community as Minister General. She is also a curate in the Diocese of Southwell and Nottingham, has written three books for BRF, and has contributed to *Quiet Spaces*.

Veronica Zundel is an Oxford graduate, writer and journalist. She lives with her husband and son in North London, where they belong to the Mennonite Church.

Andrew Jones is Archdeacon of Meirionnydd in the Diocese of Bangor. He has written *Pilgrimage: the journey to remembering our story* (BRF, 2011 and *Mary: a Gospel witness to transfiguration and liberation* (BRF, 2014).

Naomi Starkey writes...

When I was first asked become the editor of *New Daylight*, 15 years ago, it felt like an enormous challenge. I was awed by the achievements of my predecessors, Shelagh Brown and David Winter. I wondered how I would manage the intricate 'jigsaw puzzle' of contributors and contributions, covering the high days and holidays of the church calendar as well as encouraging people to engage with the whole of the Bible, some parts of which were difficult to present as daily devotional reading, to say the least!

And here I am, writing my last editorial letter, after working on 42 issues of the notes and also (since 2008) contributing readings myself. I have had the privilege of working with an amazing and stimulating assortment of writers who have patiently responded to my editorial queries and comments—and occasional demands for a major rewrite. I have also enjoyed the equal privilege of corresponding with *New Daylight* readers, who have written, emailed and sometimes phoned comments, often generous words of praise but also thought-provoking critique or helpful suggestions as to how we could improve the notes. Given the busyness of so many people's lives, it has been humbling to receive a card or letter showing how the sender has been moved, or made to think hard, by a reading. Most moving have been the times when a Bible passage and related comment have 'happened' to fall on a day of particular and sometimes painful significance for somebody, providing much-needed reassurance of God's loving presence.

My own journey has taken me on the path to ordained ministry in the Anglican Church, and my years of editing *New Daylight* have reinforced for me the importance of systematically getting to know the Bible in order to grow in faith—a discipline that will continue as a key emphasis in my church ministry. At the same time, the theological studies that formed part of my ordination training gave me fresh inspiration for my editorial role and new insights into the most familiar of Bible passages.

So it's goodbye from me, with thanks for sharing this journey with me, and wishing you every blessing as you continue your walk of faith. I am delighted to commend the Revd Sally Welch as the next editor and I look forward very much to continuing to write for the notes myself.

5

The BRF Prayer

Almighty God,
you have taught us that your word is a lamp for our feet
and a light for our path. Help us, and all who prayerfully
read your word, to deepen our fellowship with you
and with each other through your love.
And in so doing may we come to know you more fully,
love you more truly, and follow more faithfully
in the steps of your son Jesus Christ, who lives and reigns
with you and the Holy Spirit, one God for evermore.
Amen

Paul's testimony

In 2013, a video posted on the Internet went 'viral' and was watched an incredible 38 million times on the same day. Astounding as this is, it is just a hint of what is now possible in terms of communicating with a global audience, as nearly 3 billion people are connected to the Internet. What a contrast with the first century, when the fastest form of communication was a messenger on horseback. Yet, with such basic means of sending messages, in a few short decades, the news about the life, death and resurrection of Jesus Christ went 'viral'. Such was the impact of the life-transforming resurrection power of Jesus that, despite wave after wave of vicious persecution, the message of a small Jewish sect in Galilee went on to become the dominant religion of the Roman Empire.

Without doubt, one of the key figures in those first decades of dramatic growth in the Christian church was Saul of Tarsus, later known as Paul. Having grown up a Roman citizen in a strict Jewish family, it was not unusual to have two names. It is hardly surprising to find him using his Hebrew name of Saul when his religious zeal led him to persecute the early Christians. Nor is it unexpected that he would utilise his Latin name of Paul as his missionary calling increasingly took him to Gentiles and he made every effort to accommodate himself and his message to their context (1 Corinthians 9:19–23).

During the next 13 days, we are going to explore the life of Paul, mainly through his writings. We will not attempt a chronological biography, nor a detailed travelogue of his missionary journeys. Rather, by reflecting on the experiences and influences that shaped him, we shall seek to be changed into greater Christlikeness ourselves. By observing how the Lord fashioned Paul's character and used his influence, we will find encouragement and inspiration for our journey. 'The scriptures were not given to increase our knowledge, but to change our lives', 19th-century evangelist D.L. Moody is credited as saying. As we delve into Paul's life, may we heed his bold instruction to the Corinthians: 'Follow my example, as I follow the example of Christ' (1 Corinthians 11:1).

Steve Aisthorpe

The child is father of the man

'I am a Jew, born in Tarsus of Cilicia, but brought up in this city. I studied under Gamaliel and was thoroughly trained in the law of our ancestors. I was just as zealous for God as any of you are today. I persecuted the followers of this Way to their death, arresting both men and women and throwing them into prison, as the high priest and all the Council can themselves testify. I even obtained letters from them to their associates in Damascus, and went there to bring these people as prisoners to Jerusalem to be punished.'

A poem by William Wordsworth, 'The Rainbow', includes the phrase, 'The child is father of the man'. At first this seems paradoxical. On further reflection, however, it expresses a profound truth—one that helps us to understand Paul, because this man, who became the apostle to the Gentiles (Romans 11:13), was, first of all, Saul of Tarsus.

The circumstances of his early years combined to lay a foundation for what was to come. Paul's religious credentials were impeccable: he was a 'Hebrew of Hebrews' (Philippians 3:5). He spoke Hebrew and was intimately acquainted with the scriptures. He went on to study in Jerusalem under its most distinguished teacher, Gamaliel.

Paul's background supplied him with other attributes, too. Tarsus was a centre for Greek philosophy and he became familiar with Greek language and culture. It was also a hub for producing the goat's hair fabric used for tentmaking and he learned a trade (Acts 18:3).

His outstanding knowledge of the scriptures would enable him to reason in synagogues with both Jews and 'God-fearing Greeks' (Acts 17:4). Indeed, his education and upbringing would enable him to be equally at home 'in the marketplace… with those who happened to be there' (v. 17). He also inherited the status of being a Roman citizen.

In God's providence, Paul was uniquely prepared, yet, later in life, he came to see his standing and status as 'garbage' compared to all that he found in Christ (Philippians 3:8).

Prayer

Lord Jesus, help me to appreciate the ways in which you have equipped me and yet remind me that all is worthless compared with knowing you.

STEVE AISTHORPE

Blinded by the light

Meanwhile, Saul was still breathing out murderous threats against the Lord's disciples. He went to the high priest and asked him for letters to the synagogues in Damascus, so that if he found any there who belonged to the Way, whether men or women, he might take them as prisoners to Jerusalem. As he neared Damascus on his journey, suddenly a light from heaven flashed around him. He fell to the ground and heard a voice say to him, 'Saul, Saul, why do you persecute me?' 'Who are you, Lord?' Saul asked. 'I am Jesus, whom you are persecuting,' he replied. 'Now get up and go into the city, and you will be told what you must do.'

We sometimes forget that the man who began his letters with the words 'grace' and 'peace' was previously overflowing with hostility towards Christians. So abhorrent did he find the followers of 'the Way' (v. 2), that he determined to root them out and eradicate the fledgling church. Indeed, when we are told that Paul began to 'destroy' the church (Acts 8:3), the word used is an extreme one—its only other use in the Bible is to describe the ravaging of delicate vines by wild boars (Psalm 80:13).

Imagine the scene. As he approaches Damascus, inspired by religious duty, he genuinely believes he is pleasing God. What a phenomenal shock, then, as, even in the glaring midday sun (Acts 22:6), there is a more brilliant light as he comes face to face with the Jesus he assumes to be dead, but discovers is risen. As he hears his own name repeated in Jesus' native Aramaic (Acts 26:14), he suddenly comprehends how tragically misguided his zealous crusade has been.

Now the fanatical persecutor of just a moment ago needs to be led by the hand (Acts 9:8). The one who is blinded is told that he will open the eyes of others; the one plunged into darkness is appointed to turn others to light (Acts 26:18).

Reflection

'For you were once darkness, but now you are light in the Lord. Live as children of light (for the fruit of the light consists in all goodness, righteousness and truth) and find out what pleases the Lord' (Ephesians 5:8–10).

STEVE AISTHORPE

9

Significant others

In Damascus there was a disciple named Ananias. The Lord called to him in a vision, 'Ananias!' 'Yes, Lord,' he answered. The Lord told him, 'Go to the house of Judas on Straight Street and ask for a man from Tarsus named Saul, for he is praying. In a vision he has seen a man named Ananias come and place his hands on him to restore his sight.' 'Lord,' Ananias answered, 'I have heard many reports about this man and all the harm he has done to your holy people in Jerusalem. And he has come here with authority from the chief priests to arrest all who call on your name.' But the Lord said to Ananias, 'Go!'

I wonder who was most terrified. Was it the trembling disciple, summoned to meet the instigator of such brutal persecution, or the vulnerable blind man, once so sure of his actions, but now waiting in darkness to meet a person who, until a short time ago, had been an intended victim, to be dragged from his home and extradited to Jerusalem?

Despite previously being on opposite sides of a bitter religious dispute, both men had been attentive to the Lord these past three days. To Paul, the Lord had promised healing (v. 12). To Ananias, the Lord had revealed his plan for this oppressor to be his instrument to proclaim the gospel to 'the Gentiles and their kings and to the people of Israel' (9:15b).

What a relief to both of them, then, when Paul's sight returned (9:18) and they found that they had heard the Lord's command correctly. What an intensely moving moment for Paul to be addressed as 'brother' (v. 17) by one who could so easily have harboured bitterness for all the terror that Paul had inflicted.

Throughout Paul's early days as a Christian there would be those who would fear him, sceptical of his conversion (v. 26). Others, like Ananias—and Barnabas (v. 27)—recognised the work of God and became the Lord's accomplices in the formation of this man who would be central in the exponential expansion of the church.

Prayer
Lord, help me to recognise your work in those I encounter and be a collaborator in your purposes. Amen

STEVE AISTHORPE

GALATIANS 1:15–19 (NIV)

A season of solitude

But when God, who set me apart from my mother's womb and called me by his grace, was pleased to reveal his Son in me so that I might preach him among the Gentiles, my immediate response was not to consult any human being. I did not go up to Jerusalem to see those who were apostles before I was, but I went into Arabia. Later I returned to Damascus. Then after three years, I went up to Jerusalem to get acquainted with Cephas and stayed with him fifteen days. I saw none of the other apostles—only James, the Lord's brother.

Just as the other apostles were prepared for a lifetime of mission after their three years of intensive formation in the company of Jesus, so was Paul. Rather than walking the highways and byways of Galilee, Samaria and Judea with Jesus in his earthly incarnation, however, Paul spent three years in Arabia in prayerful fellowship with the risen Christ. Scholars debate whether Paul began his preaching ministry before heading to Arabia or not, but the main point seems to be that very soon after his conversion, Paul chose to withdraw.

Surely much of what Paul came to understand about the ways of God took root in that three-year period of retreat. Imagine the awe and excitement as he reflected on his intimate knowledge of the Hebrew scriptures and found the birth, life, death and resurrection of Jesus Christ writ large from beginning to end. No doubt there were also tears of regret and earnest confession as he came to terms with his misguided persecution of the first believers—and then overwhelming relief and profound release as he received the Lord's forgiveness and peace.

Like David, Moses and Jesus before him, Paul could see, in retrospect, that God had used his season of protracted obscurity in Arabia to prepare him for the particular challenges and responsibilities that were to come. Far away from the then hub of the early church, Paul learned utter dependence on God. Paul's sermons and letters, so foundational to the Christian faith, are themselves built on the deep foundations laid in these years of anonymity and seclusion.

Reflection
Advances in God's kingdom are often rooted in seasons of retreat.

STEVE AISTHORPE

A glimpse of the inner life

For through the law I died to the law so that I might live for God.
I have been crucified with Christ and I no longer live, but Christ
lives in me. The life I now live in the body, I live by faith in the Son
of God, who loved me and gave himself for me. I do not set aside
the grace of God, for if righteousness could be gained through the
law, Christ died for nothing!

Paul's letters give us tantalising glimpses of the inner revolution that
took place in those years following his encounter with Christ. Growing
up a conscientious Pharisee, he was thoroughly familiar with God's
Law. From his earliest memories he had sincerely and energetically
pursued what he thought was the only way to please God. In describing
his earlier life to the Christians in Philippi, he said that he had gone as
far as it was possible to go to make himself right with God by obeying
the Law, he could not have done more (Philippians 3:5–6), but now an
outright transformation in his understanding had occurred.

After years of trying to earn his way into God's good books, the
ridiculous futility of such an idea dawned on him and the purpose of
Christ's death became apparent. The word translated here as 'righteousness' (Galatians 2:21)—or 'justification' in some translations—was
a legal term used to declare someone innocent. It means the exact
opposite of condemnation. Paul later explained the simple yet mind-
blowing insight that changed him utterly like this: 'there is now no
condemnation for those who are in Christ Jesus' (Romans 8:1).

Whereas his life had been driven by a deep sense of religious duty,
now his unimaginable gratitude and joy fuelled an insatiable desire to
share this good news with the world—especially his own people, whose
misdirected zeal broke his heart (Romans 10:1–2). Delivered from a
fanatical obligation to the Law, he now rejoices in the personal knowledge that the one who is Lord 'lives in me' (Galatians 2:19), 'loved me'
and 'gave himself for me' (v. 20).

Prayer

*Lord Jesus, set me free from religious duty and fill me afresh with
thanksgiving for all you have done to declare me 'not guilty'. Amen*

STEVE AISTHORPE

Sent by—and with—Christ

Now in the church at Antioch there were prophets and teachers: Barnabas, Simeon called Niger, Lucius of Cyrene, Manaen (who had been brought up with Herod the tetrarch) and Saul. While they were worshipping the Lord and fasting, the Holy Spirit said, 'Set apart for me Barnabas and Saul for the work to which I have called them.' So after they had fasted and prayed, they placed their hands on them and sent them off. The two of them, sent on their way by the Holy Spirit, went down to Seleucia and sailed from there to Cyprus. When they arrived at Salamis, they proclaimed the word of God in the Jewish synagogues.

I wonder what comes to mind when you hear the words 'mission' and 'missionary'? For many people these are words loaded with misunderstandings. Traditional images tend to emphasise extremes: white men in pith helmets, large black Bible in hand, 'taking Jesus to' cannibalistic tribes or else celebrity evangelists preaching to multitudes.

In truth, the word 'mission' simply means 'sending'. From the beginning of time, God has been in the business of sending: first, his creative word and life-giving breath to create all that has been (Genesis 1—2), then a particular family to be a blessing to all families (Genesis 12:1–3) and, ultimately, his own son 'to seek and to save what was lost' (Luke 19:10). Jesus made it clear that to follow him involves being part of God's grand plan to redeem all of creation when he said, 'As the Father has sent me, I am sending you' (John 20:21).

The dynamic and cosmopolitan church in Antioch had a healthy perspective on mission. There was a realisation that mission is God's work, but, in his generosity and love, he invites us to be his accomplices. Barnabas and Saul were God's choice for a particular task and, as they moved forward in faith, the Holy Spirit guided them and demonstrated by the first of many compelling signs that they were indeed working hand in hand with God. Paul understood himself as one who was not only sent *by* Christ, but also sent *with* Christ.

Reflection

'Go… I am with you always' (Matthew 28:19–20).

STEVE AISTHORPE

A heart for his own

My friends, how I wish with all my heart that my own people might be saved! How I pray to God for them! I can assure you that they are deeply devoted to God; but their devotion is not based on true knowledge. They have not known the way in which God puts people right with himself, and instead, they have tried to set up their own way; and so they did not submit themselves to God's way of putting people right. For Christ has brought the Law to an end, so that everyone who believes is put right with God.

Love for one another is the high calling of Jesus for his followers, the hallmark of Christian community: 'As I have loved you, so you must love one another' (John 13:34). This is not a vague love for everyone in general. Rather, the love that Paul says, 'has been poured out into our hearts through the Holy Spirit' (Romans 5:5, NIV) is for particular people, including our 'own people', those God has brought into our lives, our family, friends and neighbours. So Paul, although commissioned from the very beginning to take the good news about Jesus to people of a different background from his own (Acts 9:15), discovered a deep and heartfelt concern for his own people.

Having recognised the senselessness of his own attempts to please God and discovered the magnificent truth that God himself had put all things right between them by means of Jesus, it is altogether natural that Paul's loving concern should turn to those people who walk the very same road he had been pursuing with such vigour and enthusiasm.

Even as Paul went on to become 'the apostle to the Gentiles' (Romans 11:13) and even as the Gentile churches experienced rapid growth and the Jews remained stubborn in the face of God's kindness (2:4), Paul's strategy remained, 'first for the Jew, then for the Gentile'.

Reflection

For Paul, 'my own people' were the Israelites—with their special place in God's plans. However, whatever 'my own people' means to us, we should be challenged by his intense desire for their best interests and his unwavering perseverance in reaching out to them in Christian love.

STEVE AISTHORPE

Guided by the Spirit

Paul and his companions travelled throughout the region of Phrygia and Galatia, having been kept by the Holy Spirit from preaching the word in the province of Asia. When they came to the border of Mysia, they tried to enter Bithynia, but the Spirit of Jesus would not allow them to. So they passed by Mysia and went down to Troas. During the night Paul had a vision of a man of Macedonia standing and begging him, 'Come over to Macedonia and help us.' After Paul had seen the vision, we got ready at once to leave for Macedonia, concluding that God had called us to preach the gospel to them.

It is no surprise that, after Antioch, the first stop for Paul, Barnabas and John Mark was Cyprus. Barnabas was from Cyprus (Acts 4:36) and John Mark was his cousin (Colossians 4:10), but where next?

Some have suggested that Paul had a strategic plan. It is proposed that, for tactical reasons, he focused on towns that were crossroads for important trade routes, Roman administrative centres, hubs of Greek civilisation and centres of Jewish influence. No doubt a man of Paul's intellectual prowess will have carefully considered many factors; after all, surely the Lord intends us to make use of our God-given common sense.

Paul, however, was also a man who understood that Christian leadership is, first, a matter of following. To participate in God's mission requires careful listening before anything else—not only to the rational facts, but first and foremost to the Lord himself. Sometimes the Lord's purposes were discerned through circumstances: opposition pointed to it being time to move on; openness and opportunities suggested a longer stay. In Pisidian Antioch, when crowds of Gentiles were eager to hear more and Jews were jealous and abusive, it signalled a move of emphasis to the Gentiles (Acts 14:1–6).

Paul's prayerful faithfulness led him and his companions from place to place, but occasionally God's purposes were beyond his ability to imagine and demanded direct intervention by blocking their preferred route and leading them elsewhere.

Prayer

Lord, when my way is not your way, please set me on your path. Amen

STEVE AISTHORPE

2 CORINTHIANS 11:24–28 (NIV)

A challenging perspective

Five times I received from the Jews the forty lashes minus one. Three times I was beaten with rods, once I was pelted with stones, three times I was shipwrecked, I spent a night and a day in the open sea, I have been constantly on the move. I have been in danger from rivers, in danger from bandits, in danger from my fellow Jews, in danger from Gentiles; in danger in the city, in danger in the country, in danger at sea; and in danger from false believers. I have laboured and toiled and have often gone without sleep; I have known hunger and thirst and have often gone without food; I have been cold and naked. Besides everything else, I face daily the pressure of my concern for all the churches.

When recruiting members for his 1914 expedition to Antarctica, Ernest Shackleton posted the advert, 'Men wanted for hazardous journey, small wages, bitter cold, long months of complete darkness, constant danger, safe return doubtful, honour and recognition in case of success.'

It proved to be accurate. In the history of human endeavour, few voyages have rivalled the extended hardship and anxiety faced by Shackleton's party after their ship was crushed by Antarctic ice. Compared to Paul's life, however, their struggles were short-lived and at no point did they face violent human opposition. By any comparison Paul's perseverance was remarkable. His life demonstrated that, 'Love never gives up' (1 Corinthians 13:4, THE MESSAGE).

While few are called to face the extremes of adversity that Paul encountered, following Christ does involve sacrifice and danger. When we do face difficulties, we should be encouraged that we follow the same God who gave Paul such remarkable resources of endurance, patience and joy. His experiences point to the extraordinary power of God at work in an ordinary person.

Reflection

'Every test that you have experienced is the kind that normally comes to people. But God keeps his promise, and he will not allow you to be tested beyond your power to remain firm… He will give you the strength to endure it, and so provide you with a way out' (1 Corinthians 10:13, GNB).

STEVE AISTHORPE

1 CORINTHIANS 2:1B–5 (NIV)

An unfaltering focus on Jesus

When I came to you, I did not come with eloquence or human wisdom as I proclaimed to you the testimony about God. For I resolved to know nothing while I was with you except Jesus Christ and him crucified. I came to you in weakness with great fear and trembling. My message and my preaching were not with wise and persuasive words, but with a demonstration of the Spirit's power, so that your faith might not rest on human wisdom, but on God's power.

There is a German proverb that translates as, 'The main thing is that the main thing remains the main thing'. Like most proverbs that stand the test of time, it is wise advice. In this case it is also pertinent for the church. For disciples of Christ, the main thing is, and always will be, Jesus Christ himself. So, when preaching becomes about the preacher, we have lost the plot; when worship becomes about the music, we have gone off at a tangent; when structures, traditions, hierarchies, buildings or anything else come even close to impinging on the absolute priority of Jesus Christ, we are off track.

Paul's focus on Jesus was unswerving and an inevitable consequence of who he understood himself to be. Although it is often translated as 'servant', a key word used by Paul to identify himself literally means a 'bondservant' of Christ Jesus (Romans 1:1). It refers to an employee who was paid wages and may often have had substantial skills and responsibilities, but who was totally devoted to one master, unable to abandon him to work for another. In several letters he introduces himself as 'an apostle of Jesus Christ', which, although it came to be misused as a kind of badge of rank by some (2 Corinthians 11:5), for Paul was a reminder of who had sent him and whose messenger he was: 'Paul, an apostle—sent not with a human commission nor by human authority, but by Jesus Christ and God the Father, who raised him from the dead' (Galatians 1:1, TNIV).

Prayer
Lord, please help me to focus afresh on you and put you at the centre of all I think and say and do. Amen

STEVE AISTHORPE

A passion for partnership

I always thank my God as I remember you in my prayers, because I hear about your love for all his holy people and your faith in the Lord Jesus. I pray that your partnership with us in the faith may be effective in deepening your understanding of every good thing we share for the sake of Christ. Your love has given me great joy and encouragement, because you, brother, have refreshed the hearts of the Lord's people.

When people share the same father, they are brothers or sisters. Despite his past as persecutor of the church, the first word spoken by the first Christian that Paul met after his conversion was 'Brother' (Acts 9:17). Although he sometimes needed to admonish them, there is no doubting Paul's deep love and concern for his brothers and sisters in Christ.

For Paul, following Jesus inevitably led him into a profound partnership with every other follower. Just as embracing Christ meant participating in both his sufferings and the promise of glory (Romans 8:17), so it also involved sharing in the sorrows and the joys of the Christian community. To Paul, sharing the gospel was not merely conveying a message; it involved the sharing of his whole life as he modelled the kind of radical fellowship into which people were invited: 'Because of our love for you we were ready to share with you not only the Good News from God but even our own lives' (1 Thessalonians 2:8, GNB).

It is not surprising that some of Paul's most impassioned exhortations are for believers to practise this wholehearted sharing and some of his warmest commendations are reserved for those who do so. This deep fellowship was not just a strong commonality based on shared values but also involved a practical sharing. Paul encouraged the Christians in Rome to give to brothers and sisters in need (Romans 12:13); he praised the believers in Philippi for joining in 'the giving and receiving' (Philippians 4:14). In his letter to Philemon, it is on the basis of their partnership that he beseeches him to welcome the slave Onesimus as a brother (1:17). Jesus breaks down barriers and transforms relationships.

Reflection
'All one in Christ Jesus' (Galatians 3:28).

STEVE AISTHORPE

A man of letters

Give my greetings to the brothers and sisters at Laodicea, and to Nympha and the church in her house. After this letter has been read to you, see that it is also read in the church of the Laodiceans and that you in turn read the letter from Laodicea. Tell Archippus: 'See to it that you complete the work you have received in the Lord.' I, Paul, write this greeting in my own hand. Remember my chains. Grace be with you.

Have you ever considered how diminished and diluted the New Testament would be without Paul's letters? Some are lost to us, but in God's providence we have 13 of his epistles in our Bibles. We easily take for granted much of their explanation and clarification. Without his exposition of love (1 Corinthians 13), his careful unpacking of justification (Romans 4), his stirring affirmations of hope in his reflections on the resurrection of Christ (1 Corinthians 15)—the list could go on and on—our New Testament would seem threadbare indeed.

As precious as his epistles have become to us, we do well to remember that he was writing to specific individuals and churches. The Lord had given him an intense concern for these brothers and sisters, a burden of loving care that he experienced as keenly as physical hardship or persecution (2 Corinthians 11:28).

More than anything, he longed for face-to-face fellowship with these dear people: 'Night and day we pray most earnestly that we may see you face to face and restore whatever is lacking in your faith' (1 Thessalonians 3:10, NRSV). When geographical distance, the confinement of prison or the constraints of poor health thwarted his hopes, however, he found another way—prayerfully and carefully crafted letters that radiate his affection and concern. Whether the focus of these epistles was encouragement, rebuke or difficult instruction, they consistently began, ended and were infused with grace. Written over a couple of decades, when viewed together, the letters illustrate his own journey in discipleship.

Prayer

Lord, show me the people you have given me a special concern for and give me Paul-like dedication in seeking their well-being and growth. Amen

STEVE AISTHORPE

19

2 Timothy 4:6–8 (NIV)

Finishing well

For I am already being poured out like a drink offering, and the time for my departure is near. I have fought the good fight, I have finished the race, I have kept the faith. Now there is in store for me the crown of righteousness, which the Lord, the righteous Judge, will award to me on that day—and not only to me, but also to all who have longed for his appearing.

A farmer can see a crop harvested and feel profound gratitude. A craftsman can look at a finished article and experience the satisfaction of a job well done. Many of us, however, have few opportunities to stand back and reflect on the fruit of our labours. We live in an era when the outcomes of many jobs are intangible.

Paul, too, was called to serve in ways that yielded few truly concrete results. With the benefit of two millennia of hindsight, we see that his influence was phenomenal. As Paul approached the end of his life, however, there were plenty of reasons for possibly doubting the impact of his achievements. False teaching was rife and churches he established were wrestling with a range of critical difficulties.

The words we read today are some of Paul's last recorded words. A striking fact is that they are not about achievements realised or feats accomplished. Rather, Paul finds contentment in his faithfulness. As he writes to urge young Timothy to practise endurance and servant-hearted leadership, Paul can say with confidence and candour that he has been faithful to his vocation, diligent in the responsibilities to which the Lord called him. Despite the serious errors of his early life, not least his violent persecution of the church, there is no regret: that was all forgiven long ago. Nor is there resentment that he is imprisoned: he has learned to find contentment in the most trying of circumstances (Philippians 4:12–13). More than anything, Paul knew the deep fulfilment of hearing the words, 'Well done, good and faithful servant!' (Matthew 25:21, 23).

Prayer

Lord Jesus, deliver me from fear of failure and compulsion to succeed—and grow in me the fruit of your Spirit that is patient endurance and persevering faithfulness. Amen

Steve Aisthorpe

Scattering sin's darkness

'Let God rise up and let his enemies be scattered' (Psalm 68:1). As the Easter candle is lit during the age-old vigil, the minister announces similarly, 'May the light of Christ, rising in glory, banish all darkness from our hearts and minds.'

Our theme of 'Scattering sin's darkness' is about self-examination and repentance. 'Sin' is a word that sits uncomfortably with us today, viewed in a less matter-of-fact and more lurid way due to tabloid sensationalism. In biblical understanding it is no more or less than the ways in which we fall short in living as God calls us to live. We sin because we are sinners—nothing sensational there—but (and this is sensational) God has set his heart on us even though we are sinners. He seeks to cast out the darkness of our sin so we can shine with the light of his love.

The scripture we will be covering invites self-examination in the three dimensions Jesus indicated when he said, '"You shall love the Lord your God with all your heart, and with all your soul, and with all your mind." This is the greatest and first commandment. And a second is like it: "You shall love your neighbour as yourself"' (Matthew 22:37–39).

We start by considering forgiveness, then lament our failure to love (Lamentations 3), then move on to the call to humility (1 Peter 5) before thinking about the Father's love (Luke 15), who is capable of restoring our joy (Psalm 51). We next look at sins against others, such as judging them (Matthew 7), the invitation to grow more fruitful in love (Luke 19; 1 Corinthians 13; Galatians 5) and the call to perfection (Matthew 5).

There are special readings for Holy Cross Day and Yom Kippur, the Jewish Day of Atonement, when we focus on the work of God's redeeming love, as the good news of God's love and forgiveness is pivotal to any consideration of human shortcomings.

'Scattering sin's darkness' is the work of the Holy Spirit in lives open to him in word and sacrament, prayer and Christian fellowship. Through our reflection, may we gain 'the light of the knowledge of the glory of God in the face of Jesus Christ' (2 Corinthians 4:6).

John Twisleton

21

Source of forgiveness

When they came to the place that is called The Skull, they crucified Jesus there with the criminals, one on his right and one on his left. Then Jesus said, 'Father, forgive them; for they do not know what they are doing.'... It was now about noon, and darkness came over the whole land until three in the afternoon, while the sun's light failed; and the curtain of the temple was torn in two. Then Jesus, crying with a loud voice, said, 'Father, into your hands I commend my spirit.' Having said this, he breathed his last.

Today has special significance for me as a priest of the Society of the Holy Cross, a fraternity devoted to holiness and sacrificial service, as it is our patronal feast day, when we celebrate the death of Jesus. Holy Cross Day originated in the fourth-century worship of the Jerusalem church in the early days of legal Christianity under Constantine.

The lifting up of Christ on the cross draws us like a magnet towards his divine mercy. It is represented in Luke's account by the Lord's plea for his executioners, 'Father, forgive them.' That plea ascends for us and for all from the foundation of the world to its consummation. Like any word of God, it has a transformative power and we find that power in confession and absolution.

As a priest, one of my greatest privileges is to pronounce words of absolution to penitent sinners from Christ's cross by his authority vested in me, as well as hearing those words said to me when I go to confession. Although the forgiveness won for us by the cross and resurrection can come through prayer or scripture, the one-to-one encounter with a minister of absolution provides powerful assurance.

The most effective Christians are those who live with knowledge of their need of the divine mercy revealed on the 'Holy Cross'. There atonement was made once for all between sinful humans and their holy Creator through that lifting up of Christ as the source of forgiveness.

Prayer

We adore you, O Christ, and we bless you, because by your Holy Cross you have redeemed the world.

Prayer at first station of the cross
JOHN TWISLETON

Let us return to the Lord

The steadfast love of the Lord never ceases, his mercies never come to an end; they are new every morning; great is your faithfulness. 'The Lord is my portion,' says my soul, 'therefore I will hope in him'… Let us test and examine our ways, and return to the Lord.

Sin is failure to love God, neighbour and self—the three dimensions that define our existence and frame our lifelong learning. In all three dimensions, there are shadows to be scattered by our coming into the light of the Lord. As the psalmist wrote, 'Your word is a lamp to my feet and a light to my path' (119:105).

Our sinful condition blinds us to both our sin and divine mercy. Very often it makes a burden for us that we need not carry, such as the feeling of wounded pride we have when we mess up. This is a shadow of the reality, which is, in truth, the failure to reach outside of ourselves in generous love—and it is this failure that we should lament as it affects God and neighbour as well as, ultimately, ourselves.

The book of Lamentations is set at a time of great sorrow for God's people as they see Jerusalem despoiled. In Holy Week, the church uses this book to express her lament at the despoiling of her Lord and Saviour Jesus Christ in his passion. 'Let us test and examine our ways, and return to the Lord' (v. 40), is the invitation, as is the invitation of this series of passages, for 'The steadfast love of the Lord never ceases, his mercies never come to an end; they are new every morning' (v. 22–23).

These verses from Lamentations shine like jewels in its overall desolate tone, which speaks of times that sounded like the end of the world. God's assurance is clear, scattering the darkness of remorse at the unfaithful acts that triggered the calamity of exile. As morning follows night, he intimates, so my love will be made evident to those who keep humble faith in me.

Prayer

May the light of Christ, rising in glory, banish all darkness
from our hearts and minds.

Easter candle blessing, the Service of Light

JOHN TWISLETON

1 PETER 5:5B–9 (NRSV)

Humble yourself

All of you must clothe yourselves with humility in your dealings with one another, for 'God opposes the proud, but gives grace to the humble.' Humble yourselves therefore under the mighty hand of God, so that he may exalt you in due time. Cast all your anxiety on him, because he cares for you. Discipline yourselves; keep alert. Like a roaring lion your adversary the devil prowls around, looking for someone to devour. Resist him, steadfast in your faith, for you know that your brothers and sisters throughout the world are undergoing the same kinds of suffering.

The first letter of Peter was written during a situation of persecution when Christians were suffering hugely. As the writer indicates, their keeping short accounts with God and one another is the more urgent when a roaring adversary is at hand. As scripture makes plain elsewhere, the devil's main power is deception, by means of which he fuels anxiety and distrust in God in the face of calamity and so weakens the body of Christ in the face of its opponents.

Humility is truth. Before God, human beings stand like pots before the potter. To imagine we are the source of our own lives is a delusion at the root of the sin of pride, highlighted at the start of Genesis as the cause of our downfall. How better to deal with pride than by cultivating the opposite quality—humility—which is put forward in these verses as a most honourable thing to do.

Self-display seems an inevitable part of communication with God and neighbour, but contains what spiritual writers warn us off doing, namely 'vain speaking'. Humility is a clothing of speech that flows from listening to and centring our lives on others, and flees from vain self-display as from fire. The words of 1 Peter 5 could be a good incentive to examine recent conversations so as to identify how balanced they were.

Prayer

Lord, of your great goodness, make known to me, and take from my heart, every kind and form and degree of pride. Awaken in me the depth of humility that makes me able to receive your Holy Spirit. Amen

Adapted from Andrew Murray, *Humility* (F. Revell, 1910), p. 99

JOHN TWISLETON

The prodigal's return

[The younger son] set off and went to his father. But while he was still far off, his father saw him and was filled with compassion; he ran and put his arms around him and kissed him. Then the son said to him, 'Father, I have sinned against heaven and before you; I am no longer worthy to be called your son.' But the father said to his slaves, 'Quickly, bring out a robe—the best one—and put it on him; put a ring on his finger and sandals on his feet. And get the fatted calf and kill it, and let us eat and celebrate; for this son of mine was dead and is alive again; he was lost and is found!' And they began to celebrate.

In Luke 15, Jesus tells us of a lost sheep, a lost coin and then, most graphically of a lost son. Throughout, the joy of their finding is a pointer to God's joy at embracing the lost who are ready to be found. The son was ready, having consumed all his resources, to be made a slave in his former household. No sooner had he voiced his words of apology than his father drowned those words with lavish deeds, giving him a robe, ring and banquet.

'For God so loved the world that he gave his only Son' (John 3:16). The parable of the prodigal's return expresses that love, as does the sacrament of reconciliation (confession) in which penitent sinners 'arise and go to their Father'. The story demonstrates how God's search for us trumps ours for him again and again.

It is a truth I try to convey to many seekers after truth whom I stumble across in our confused society. The truth is indeed something we seek, but, on account of the Christian revelation, we can add that it also seeks us—and loves and awaits our homecoming!

In the light of his truth, we see ourselves both as we are and as, in his great mercy, he destines us to become.

Prayer

Lord Jesus Christ, Son of God, have mercy on me, a sinner.

The Jesus Prayer
JOHN TWISLETON

Restoration of joy

Have mercy on me, O God, according to your steadfast love; according to your abundant mercy blot out my transgressions. Wash me thoroughly from my iniquity, and cleanse me from my sin... Create in me a clean heart, O God, and put a new and right spirit within me. Do not cast me away from your presence, and do not take your holy spirit from me. Restore to me the joy of your salvation, and sustain in me a willing spirit.

The striking fervour of Psalm 51 moves us to lament the enormity of sin and want to ascend to the heights of divine mercy. Its traditional context is after Nathan confronts King David with his sins of adultery and murder (2 Samuel 12:1–13). To pray this psalm is to capture something more of what it means to be penitent—and the miracle of God's mercy. The writer cannot wait to be cleansed, such is his sense of spiritual uncleanliness.

Gregorio Allegri's famous choral setting of *Miserere* (the Latin title for this psalm) captures this hopeful ascent from the depths in its remarkable treble parts. These represent the heartfelt cry of the individual who is, even so, confident God will hear that cry. For all our failings, God is ever capable of lending us his mercy, forgiveness and joy: '… do not take your holy spirit from me. Restore to me the joy of your salvation' (Psalm 51:11). In those words lie the secret of joy, which is no passing emotion but the presence of God alongside us as we work at ongoing repentance allied to determined faith.

In Psalm 51, we capture a spiritual determination that flows in confidence and deep humility from a vision of God. The serious sin of the one traditionally considered its author, King David, like that of the New Testament hero Paul in aiding Stephen's murder (Acts 7:58–60), is a sort of encouragement to us. The God of the Bible is one who draws us towards himself by setting before us his mercy, which brings us, penitent, up from our sins, however great, into his infectious joy.

Reflection
'In your presence there is fullness of joy' (Psalm 16:11b).

John Twisleton

Judging others

[Jesus said] 'Do not judge, so that you may not be judged. For with the judgement you make you will be judged, and the measure you give will be the measure you get. Why do you see the speck in your neighbour's eye, but do not notice the log in your own eye? Or how can you say to your neighbour, "Let me take the speck out of your eye", while the log is in your own eye? You hypocrite, first take the log out of your own eye, and then you will see clearly to take the speck out of your neighbour's eye.'

Today we move from addressing sin against God to reflecting on sin against neighbour. In summarising the new law as the call to love God and neighbour as oneself, Jesus redefines sin, which is breaking God's commandments, as failure in these three dimensions of love. We are called to address our failure by coming to the Father of mercy and seeking cooperation with his grace of forgiveness and healing.

'Do not judge, so that you may not be judged' (v. 1). Those words, so emphasised by Christ in his teaching as well as in the prayer he taught us (6:9–13), are most severe. They come from one who knows more than any the seriousness of the human tendency to play God. This passage, like most of the Sermon on the Mount, is shock treatment. If only we felt its shocking power nearer to those moments when a judgemental spirit gains purchase within us!

The discipline of self-examination, in which we look at our relationship with God, neighbour and self, helps identify negative attitudes that lie behind our sinful failure to love. Sometimes we see in such an examination, behind the strength of a judgemental attitude, reluctance to judge or address within ourselves the very failing that upsets us in our neighbour. Giving that failing within ourselves to God, confessing it and receiving his forgiveness, is discovered as a removal of the 'log' that Christ says hinders our seeing things as they really are, as he sees them.

Prayer

Our Father, forgive us our trespasses as we forgive those who trespass against us and lead us not into temptation but deliver us from evil. Amen

JOHN TWISLETON

Let there be love

If I have all faith, so as to remove mountains, but do not have love, I am nothing… Love is patient; love is kind; love is not envious or boastful or arrogant or rude. It does not insist on its own way; it is not irritable or resentful; it does not rejoice in wrongdoing, but rejoices in the truth. It bears all things, believes all things, hopes all things, endures all things. Love never ends.

There is something reassuring about Paul's letters to Corinth in that 'all human nature is there'. There was as much sin in the early church as there is today, much falling short in love for God and neighbour, in the form of divisive spirit, sexual sin, spiritual pride and so on. 1 Corinthians 13 is set between two other chapters on the gifts of the Holy Spirit, notably 'tongues'. Paul affirms these gifts while appealing for their right use in building up the church in love.

Love, truth and empowerment are three essentials for right living. The gifts of the Holy Spirit bring empowerment to live in love, obedient to the truth that is in Jesus. Only in his sinless life do the three flow perfectly together, whereas we, like the Corinthians, fall short in that balancing act. We lack love to 'rejoice in the truth', our spiritual gifting fails as a result of our being 'boastful and arrogant' with it or we fail to seek empowerment 'to bear all things'.

This passage is a popular choice for marriage services, with its description of love as something that goes deeper than emotion and sexual chemistry. In its ultimate revelation, love is irrevocable, meaning that it is a gift never to be called back, as shown to us in the blood, sweat and tears of Good Friday. The one who calls us to love provides supreme demonstration of its truth and the empowerment it gives to live by that same truth. To overcome sin, which is failure in love, we need humility to seek his empowerment day by day.

Prayer

Lord, you have taught us that all our doings without love are worth nothing: send your Holy Spirit and pour into our hearts that most excellent gift of love… without which whosoever lives is counted dead before you.

From the Collect for the Second Sunday after Trinity

JOHN TWISLETON

Zacchaeus the penitent

Zacchaeus stood there and said to the Lord, 'Look, half of my possessions, Lord, I will give to the poor; and if I have defrauded anyone of anything, I will pay back four times as much.' Then Jesus said to him, 'Today salvation has come to this house, because he too is a son of Abraham. For the Son of Man came to seek out and to save the lost.'

There is something endearing about Zacchaeus—the little man who climbed a tree to see Jesus, only to find himself the centre of attention as a result of the Lord attending to him in love—even if his descent from that tree is in some ways seen as him being taken down a peg. Jesus validates Zacchaeus, although he is a social outcast, in a fashion typical of our Lord's ongoing demonstration of love that has no partiality.

The Lord's munificence to Zacchaeus is mirrored by his confession of sin and his ample penance: 'Half of my possessions, Lord, I will give to the poor; and if I have defrauded anyone of anything, I will pay back four times as much' (v. 8). This incident is reminiscent of Jesus' comment on the woman who anointed him, saying that her generosity reflected her sense of being forgiven much (Luke 7:47).

So many biblical heroes demonstrably grow in love as a result of their encounters with the God who 'came to seek out and to save the lost' (v. 10). Think of King David, associated with beautiful psalms of penitence following his adultery being found out and forgiven by God. Then there is Paul, former persecutor of Christians, who boldly states, 'I received mercy, so that in me, as the foremost, Jesus Christ might display the utmost patience, making me an example to those who would come to believe in him for eternal life' (1 Timothy 1:16).

'Today salvation has come to this house' (Luke 19:9), Jesus said to Zacchaeus. How can that truth be ours today? From the sense of mercy obtained, which we hand on to others.

Reflection

When all thy mercies, O my God, my rising soul surveys, transported with the view I'm lost in wonder, love and praise.

Joseph Addison, 1712

JOHN TWISLETON

GALATIANS 5:22–25 (NRSV)

Let there be fruit

The fruit of the Spirit is love, joy, peace, patience, kindness, generosity, faithfulness, gentleness, and self-control. There is no law against such things. And those who belong to Christ Jesus have crucified the flesh with its passions and desires. If we live by the Spirit, let us also be guided by the Spirit.

It was a Mirfield Father, a member of the Anglican Community of the Resurrection in Yorkshire, who first taught me the value of these verses in the ongoing discipline of self-examination. Father Silvanus wanted to help me seek a positive focus at a time when I was somewhat overwhelmed by a sense of spiritual inadequacy. 'Instead of looking at the works of the flesh, seek out in your life the fruit of the Holy Spirit', he advised. 'Take stock regularly of the growth of love, joy, peace and so on that is evidently happening and your thanksgiving will water its growth.'

We are called to love God with our whole heart, mind, soul and strength and our neighbour as ourselves. Sin is falling short in that calling. Whereas specific sins need to be identified—to give to God in our repentance as we seek his forgiveness—in order to achieve balanced self-examination, we need to be mindful of the good that is being achieved in our lives as well as the bad.

'Two men looked out from prison bars. One saw mud, the other stars' (variously attributed). Looking at ourselves is so often like looking at mud! We need the sort of corrective suggested by scripture in its affirmation of fruit growing out of the mud, which is not of our making but the result of us inviting God's Holy Spirit to dwell deep within us.

'And those who belong to Christ Jesus have crucified the flesh with its passions and desires' (v. 24), Paul says to the Galatians, encouraging decisive action to uproot the weeds of sin. He goes on more positively to affirm the soul as being, nevertheless, God's garden: 'If we live by the Spirit, let us also be guided by the Spirit' (v. 25).

Prayer

Come, Holy Spirit, fill the hearts of your faithful servants and bless in them the growth of love, joy, peace, patience, kindness, generosity, faithfulness, gentleness, and self-control.

JOHN TWISLETON

Scapegoat

Aaron shall lay both his hands on the head of the live goat, and confess over it all the iniquities of the people of Israel, and all their transgressions, all their sins, putting them on the head of the goat, and sending it away into the wilderness by means of some-one designated for the task. The goat shall bear on itself all their iniquities to a barren region; and the goat shall be set free in the wilderness.

Today, the Jewish community marks the solemn day of Yom Kippur, the Day of Atonement (which began at sundown yesterday). I knew a secular Jewish businessman, who was never at synagogue on the sabbath, yet certain to turn out for the epic demand of Yom Kippur—although he took a newspaper to read! In his relative cynicism, he still judged cele-bration of that day to have cancelling power over his shortcomings.

Our passage from Leviticus 16, which is read in synagogues today, tells of the scapegoat. In the liturgical celebration, rather as in the Christian celebration of the Passion of Jesus, there is recollection of our sins and faith in God's power to carry them away. It is, for Christians, a foreshadowing of what was to come in the death of the 'Lamb of God who takes away the sin of the world' (John 1:29).

As a priest, I have the privilege of celebrating one-to-one personal atonement with penitent sinners. In the Anglican rite, the priest sits behind the altar rail as people kneel to list their sins before the cross. In pronouncing individual absolution, I speak as if from the cross by Christ's authority, in terms of his carrying away of the sins confessed. What the Lord bore on Good Friday was the weight of all sins ever com-mitted, a carrying that lightens the load of everyone who comes to him to seek forgiveness. The scapegoat of Leviticus, meaningful to both Jews and Christians, looks forward to Calvary, just as the rite of sacramental confession looks back to God's provision for every age and place in the perfect offering of his Son.

Prayer
Lamb of God, you take away the sins of the world; grant us peace.

Agnus Dei
JOHN TWISLETON

MATTHEW 5:43–45, 48 (NRSV)

Be perfect in love

[Jesus said] 'You have heard that it was said, "You shall love your neighbour and hate your enemy." But I say to you, Love your enemies and pray for those who persecute you, so that you may be children of your Father in heaven; for he makes his sun rise on the evil and on the good, and sends rain on the righteous and on the unrighteous... Be perfect, therefore, as your heavenly Father is perfect.'

In his Gospel, Matthew presents Christ as a new Moses, giving a new Law with near impossible commandments, such as this call to love our persecutors. It can be questioned whether the old covenant made hatred of enemies so explicit or not, given texts such as Proverbs 25:21–22: 'If your enemies are hungry, give them bread to eat; and if they are thirsty, give them water to drink; for you will heap coals of fire on their heads, and the Lord will reward you.'

It seems it was less the text than the interpretation of the Law in our Lord's day that jarred with him. The kingdom of God is to have no second-class citizens. Everyone is loved equally by its king so those who want to espouse perfection must renounce all contempt for others. Such teaching is in tension with any call to hate God's enemies, representing, rather, an obligation to love sinful people, while still acknowledging the falling-short of their sin.

To flee sin is the other side of building yearning for God in ourselves and in others, so that victory over our enemies actually involves their conversion to God, no less. To be perfect, or like God, is to love all that is simply because it is—a tough call for a mere mortal!

The Sermon on the Mount is a conscience awakener. The philosopher Søren Kierkegaard compared it to setting one's alarm clock half an hour early, to ensure you do not get up late. We need its high call, but also discernment so that the best it presents does not undermine the more pragmatic working for good that Christian life is mainly about.

Reflection

How well do I balance God's call to be perfect with the lesser good of doing the best I can?

JOHN TWISLETON

God knows my heart

O Lord, you have searched me and known me. You know when I sit down and when I rise up; you discern my thoughts from far away. You search out my path and my lying down, and are acquainted with all my ways. Even before a word is on my tongue, O Lord, you know it completely. You hem me in, behind and before, and lay your hand upon me. Such knowledge is too wonderful for me; it is so high that I cannot attain it… Search me, O God, and know my heart; test me and know my thoughts. See if there is any wicked way in me, and lead me in the way everlasting.

In this series of passages on self-examination, Psalm 139 must stand pre-eminent, with its affirmation that we are known by God and, therefore, in principle, can know ourselves once we are granted a measure of that knowledge. Calvin was one great Christian teacher who presented the knowledge of God and ourselves as being quite inseparable.

The English mystical writer Francis Thompson (1859–1907) makes a commentary on this psalm in his poem, 'The hound of heaven'. He makes a strange comparison between a hound's pursuit of a hare and God's gracious pursuit of the soul, which ends with its turning towards the love following after it. This comparison echoes the psalmist's words: 'You search out my path and my lying down, and are acquainted with all my ways… Search me, O God, and know my heart' (vv. 3, 23).

Once again, the scriptures serve to prompt self-examination by reminding us that God's search for us is the ground of both our search for him and for ourselves. Contemplating the wonder of our being, as Psalm 139 invites, lifts us towards the one who made us, sees us through and through and loves us through and through.

Today's passage is one of my favourite starting points for self-examination as it affirms what we read elsewhere in scripture, that 'in your [God's] light we see light' (Psalm 36:9b).

Prayer

O Love that wilt not let me go, I rest my weary soul in thee; I give thee back the life I owe, that in thine ocean depths its flow may richer, fuller be.

George Matheson, 1882

JOHN TWISLETON

Perfect peace

> Those of steadfast mind you keep in peace—in peace because they trust in you. Trust in the Lord for ever, for in the Lord God you have an everlasting rock.

It was Samuel Sebastian Wesley's beautiful anthem setting of these words that first impressed them on me. The words and songs of liturgy are given for both God's glory and our own well-being. You can breathe in the peace of Isaiah's words and Wesley's anthem, but that peace can quickly evaporate as we leave church to enter challenging situations! This is the case unless our worship flows in and out of our lives, the faith we profess and our adherence to its ethical implications.

The 'steadfast mind' (v. 3) holds itself to the word of God, the trust in whom places us on 'an everlasting rock' (v. 4). It is about having a mind informed by scripture and the will to hold to that security in God through the storms of life. We are told to look to the Lord and be radiant (Psalm 34:5) and that looking has to be a decisive business, as so often the attention of mind and emotions are overtaken by all else that comes our way in the course of daily life.

Like football players, we are called to 'keep our eyes on the ball', which, for Christians, is a matter of attending to Jesus continually as life moves forward. As we attend to Jesus and keep our eyes on him, we welcome peace passing human understanding, even in the most severe of trials.

Self-examination is led by the will and starts with attention to what is the journey of the Christian life, particularly how much our wills are, in fact, collaborating with the Lord. Loss of peace is the classic indicator that we are travelling alone, the joy of the Lord becoming distant from us and our eyes more on the problems than on his provision.

Prayer

Lord, we are restless until we rest in you. Grant us a will directed towards you and hearts set in yours, so that your peace permeates our very being, flowing out to pacify the disquiet around us. We ask this in the name of Jesus who is our rock and our salvation. Amen

JOHN TWISLETON

Praise, my soul

Bless the Lord, O my soul, and all that is within me, bless his holy name. Bless the Lord, O my soul, and do not forget all his benefits—who forgives all your iniquity, who heals all your diseases, who redeems your life from the Pit, who crowns you with steadfast love and mercy, who satisfies you with good as long as you live so that your youth is renewed like the eagle's.

Psalm 103 is a great witness to God's sovereignty, forgiveness and fatherly care, so I have often either received or commended it in the context of sacramental confession. It contains graphic images such as, 'as far as the east is from the west, so far he removes our transgressions from us' (v. 12). Henry Lyte paraphrased this psalm into what remains to this day a very popular hymn, 'Praise, my soul, the King of heaven'.

Lyte captures the sense of the Psalm's opening paragraph in the words 'ransomed, healed, restored, forgiven', which sum up four aspects of the benefits God provides for us in Jesus Christ, 'who forgives all your iniquity, who heals all your diseases, who redeems your life from the Pit, who crowns you with steadfast love and mercy'. The darkness cast from us is that of sin, sickness and desolation, which are overcome by Christ's work when it becomes operative in our lives.

The psalm affirms forgiveness, healing and deliverance as being in the heart of God, whose power is able to overcome all sin, all sickness and bondage. We cannot live in the world without experiencing these negatives, but the redeeming love of God has the power to energise what are now the church's ministries of forgiveness, healing and deliverance. These ministries are linked, so that seeking forgiveness for habitual sins begs the question, should we not seek healing to tackle the source of our frailty instead? Similarly, our welcoming of God's deliverance from the things that bind us is linked to our fuller repentance and openness to being made whole.

Reflection

Psalm 103 invites us to count our blessings and surprise ourselves
at how much God is actually at work in our lives, despite all the ways in
which we fall short.

JOHN TWISLETON

Caring for the creatures

There are 93 different types of animal mentioned in the Bible, but only one human race. Animals were created before humanity and provided the original example of how to live together in harmony. It is through humanity, rather than through the animals, that sin came into the world and it was sin that made Cain kill Abel because he was jealous that God preferred Abel's offering to his. The serpent notwithstanding, animals did not cause the problems in the world—that was the lot of humanity. We are often inclined to view animals with a little bit of jealousy almost, which we could interpret as a longing for how things might have been in the past. It is surely not a coincidence that in the bookshops at Christmas approximately one third of the books on display are animal picture books!

The Bible shows that God made his covenant with animals as well as human beings. Human and non-human animals have the same origin in God. Francis of Assisi is reputed to have said that animals 'had the same source as himself'. In God's ideal world, human beings live in harmony with animals. The Garden of Eden, in which the man and the woman lived in peace and harmony with animals, demonstrates this ideal world and the state of affairs that we should work towards.

Having said that, the Bible talks more about what animals can do for us than what we can do for them. Animals appear at crucial points to keep the Bible story moving. Which animal made a disciple aware of his sin? A rooster (Mark 14:72). Which animal provided Jesus with money to pay taxes? A fish (Matthew 17:27). Which animals fed Elijah during the famine? Ravens (1 Kings 17:2–4). Which animal did Samson kill and later found honey in the carcass? A lion (Judges 14:5–8).

God's love is intended not just for human beings but also for all living creatures. Christians should treat every sentient animal according to its intrinsic God-given worth, not according to its perceived usefulness. If we do this, we will achieve a far greater spiritual appreciation of the worth of creation and the value of the world in which we live.

Bob Mayo

How it was supposed to be

In the beginning God created the heavens and the earth... And God said, 'Let the water teem with living creatures, and let birds fly above the earth across the vault of the sky'... And God said, 'Let the land produce living creatures according to their kinds: the livestock, the creatures that move along the ground, and the wild animals, each according to its kind.' And it was so... Then God said, 'Let us make mankind in our image, in our likeness, so that they may rule over the fish in the sea and the birds in the sky, over the livestock and all the wild animals, and over all the creatures that move along the ground.' So God created mankind in his own image, in the image of God he created them; male and female he created them.

God created animals to be our partners and so human responsibility for the created order should be seen as a joint venture with the animals rather than domination and exploitation of them. John Berger writes that animals have helped humanity to understand who and how they are in the world. The eyes of an animal, when they considered a human being, were attentive and wary. In returning their gaze, human beings became aware of their responsibility towards the created order—we, the animals' natural predators, have had to learn to care for the earth and its inhabitants, and animals have been our teachers.

We could argue that this relationship has been broken by the taking of animals into zoos. What counts in this reconfigured relationship is that the animals are now seen and known by us (rather than we by them). Even though many zoos are now also centres for the breeding and conservation of endangered species, the significance of that look between animal and humanity, which may have played a crucial role in the development of society, has been lost. Animals are now always the observed. Zoos were surely never a part of God's created world order.

Reflection

How can we be confident that any animals in captivity are there for their own well-being and not simply for the entertainment of the public?

BOB MAYO

Consider the sparrow

[Jesus said] 'Are not two sparrows sold for a penny? Yet not one of them will fall to the ground outside your Father's care. And even the very hairs of your head are all numbered. So don't be afraid; you are worth more than many sparrows... Are not five sparrows sold for two pennies? Yet not one of them is forgotten by God.'

In the overall narrative, of which our verses from Matthew are a part, Jesus tells the disciples what will happen to them after his death. They will be betrayed, hated and persecuted, yet they are not to be afraid: they must take their inspiration from the birds. If the sparrows are within the love and care of God, then how much more will the disciples be? At first reading it could appear to be a strange way to offer encouragement: in our society, if we wanted to encourage people through difficult times we might use the example of someone courageous or famous. But Jesus uses the example of a sparrow to represent security and freedom. The birds illustrate a life free from anxiety, exemplifying the trust in God that the disciples would need to show when, in the days of the early church, they faced difficulty, disillusionment or danger.

When we read these verses 2000 years later we see that once again we need to learn such lessons. We may not be persecuted for our faith but we still have to learn not to take ourselves too seriously and to trust in God—and animals can help us to learn this lesson. If we compare the two parallel verses we see that in Luke there is an extra bird thrown in for free! In Matthew you get two sparrows for a penny but in Luke you get five sparrows for two pennies: the sparrow is so small and insignificant that you buy one and get one free. If God's love is as real for the bargain sparrow as it is for us, then we should learn to give thanks for the life that we have been given.

Reflection

How can we learn from animals and other living creatures to live our lives free from anxiety?

BOB MAYO

Both innocent and shrewd

[Jesus said] 'I am sending you out like sheep among wolves. Therefore be as shrewd as snakes and as innocent as doves.'

A verse with four animals in two sentences shows the extent to which scripture abounds with references to the animal kingdom. Jesus tells his disciples that, after his death, they will be hated and persecuted because of his name (Matthew 24:9). He tells them that he is sending them out as sheep among wolves, which brings to mind Isaiah's vision of the messianic era, which says that the 'wolf will live with the lamb' (Isaiah 11:6).

Referring to the disciples as sheep also highlights the dangers that they will face in their mission. Normally, a shepherd would protect his sheep from wolves, but Jesus is sending his 'sheep' out to be surrounded by wolves. In the second set of animal images, we find the unlikely combination of a snake and a dove—unlikely because, just as the wolf is a natural predator to the sheep, so also is the snake to the dove. Jesus, however, wants the disciples to be shrewd like snakes in how they deal with the people who mean them harm, but innocent like doves in how they trust in God.

Shrewdness is a quality praised elsewhere in the Gospels. In one of Jesus' parables, the master commended the dishonest manager because he had acted shrewdly (Luke 16:8). In linking the two sets of animals together, Jesus is making his disciples aware in a vivid way of the difficult days of persecution that lie ahead. He is saying that, just as a sheep is at the mercy of a wolf and a dove a snake, so also will they be at the hands of people who seek their death. It makes the point dramatically to the disciples that they will need to keep their wits about them. Being shrewd in the world, but still innocent in trusting God, is described elsewhere in scripture as the need for believers to be in the world but not of the world (John 17:14–15).

Reflection
How can we be wise and shrewd in the way we relate to others, but innocent and trusting in the way we related to God?

BOB MAYO

Creation redeemed

The wolf will live with the lamb, the leopard will lie down with the goat, the calf and the lion and the yearling together; and a little child will lead them... The infant will play near the cobra's den, and the young child will put its hand into the viper's nest. They will neither harm nor destroy on all my holy mountain, for the earth will be filled with the knowledge of the Lord as the waters cover the sea.

This passage from Isaiah answers the question asked by anyone who has lost a much-loved pet: 'What happens to animals after they die?' In this passage, Isaiah says that animals will be a part of the new creation following the return of Christ.

We love our pets and often consider them to be members of the family. The prophet Nathan told King David a parable of a poor man for whom this was also the case. He had nothing except a little female lamb, which grew up together with him and his children: 'It shared his food, drank from his cup and even slept in his arms. It was like a daughter to him' (2 Samuel 12:3).

So, do dogs, cats, horses and other pets go to heaven? While the Bible does not come straight out and say, 'Yes', it implies, in its discussion of the redemption of God's creation, that our pets will be present in the new heaven and new earth. Revelation (19:11) says that when Jesus returns to the earth, it will be with his army of saints on white horses. God is planning on restoring his creation and that work of restoration will also include animals. Creation itself will be delivered from the burden of corruption into the glorious liberty of the children of God (Romans 8:20–21). Just as animals were a part of God's untainted original creation, so they will be part of the world and life when he makes everything new, freed from the corruption of sin and death.

Reflection

If animals are a part of God's triumphant new creation, how much more can we appreciate them as our companions in the here and now?

BOB MAYO

Even the smallest creatures

Free yourself, like a gazelle from the hand of the hunter, like a bird from the snare of the fowler. Go to the ant, you sluggard; consider its ways and be wise! It has no commander, no overseer or ruler, yet it stores its provisions in summer and gathers its food at harvest.

This passage uses three different animals to illustrate qualities that should be apparent in the life of a believer. Ants, gazelles and birds might not naturally be bracketed together, but each exhibits qualities from which we can learn. Ants show diligence and forethought, while the bird and the gazelle free themselves from traps that have been set for them.

An ant's nest is a hive of activity, as the tireless little workers toil together for the good of the whole. This image reminds us that we should live our lives with the same energy and determination as do ants. As well as being hardworking, we should also, like a gazelle escaping the hand of the hunter or a bird the snare of the trapper, through God's grace free ourselves from all that is oppressive and deadening, so that we can embrace fully the life that is ours to live.

There are opportunities for good works everywhere. As the quote attributed to John Wesley says, 'Do all the good you can; by all the means you can; in all the ways you can; in all the places you can; at all the times you can; to all the people you can—as long as ever you can.'

There are many opportunities for us to grow in our faith and love of Christ. Paul wrote about how we should 'continue to work out [our] salvation with fear and trembling' (Philippians 2:12). There are also constant reasons for us to be thankful to God. As Paul wrote in another letter, we give thanks 'in all circumstances', as this is indeed God's will for us (1 Thessalonians 5:18). Animals are uncomplicated: they delight in the life that they have, and so also should we.

Reflection

Give thanks for the lessons that we can learn from living creatures—no matter how seemingly insignificant they are.

BOB MAYO

Companions and teachers

[Job replied] 'But ask the animals, and they will teach you, or the birds in the sky, and they will tell you; or speak to the earth, and it will teach you, or let the fish in the sea inform you. Which of all these does not know that the hand of the Lord has done this? In his hand is the life of every creature and the breath of all mankind. Does not the ear test words as the tongue tastes food?'

This passage tells us that animals are our teachers and not simply our companions. I have two special animal teachers—miniature long-haired dachshunds (Sam and Tilly).

Their first gift to me is unconditional acceptance. The height of their ambition is either to sit on my lap or lick my face. This is 'unconditional positive regard', a term coined by the humanist Carl Rogers, meaning blanket acceptance and support of a person regardless of what they say or do. Rogers believes that such regard is essential to healthy human development.

Sam and Tilly's second gift is that they teach me to not hurry but take time over what I am doing. A walk that might otherwise have taken 15 minutes can take twice as long as they sniff and bark their way through the world that they are discovering.

The Little Prince, in Antoine de Saint-Exupéry's fable of the same name (1943), also learns about the importance of time from an animal. He lives on a small planet with three volcanoes and one plant. Although he travels from home and finds that people (adults) are involved in matters of great consequence, there is nothing so important to him as tending his rose plant back on his own planet. He meets a fox who explains to him why this is so: 'It is the time that you have wasted on your rose that makes your rose so important… It is only with the heart that one can see rightly; what is essential is invisible to the eye.'

Which have been the best animal teachers in your life and what have you learned?

Reflection

How are we able to learn from the animals and give, where appropriate, unconditional positive regard and take time over what we do?

BOB MAYO

Animal caring

Balaam was riding on his donkey, and his two servants were with him. When the donkey saw the angel of the Lord standing in the road with a drawn sword in his hand, it turned off the road into a field. Balaam beat it to get it back on the road... It lay down under Balaam, and he was angry and beat it with his staff... Then the Lord opened Balaam's eyes, and he saw the angel of the Lord... So he bowed low and fell face down... The angel of the Lord asked him, 'Why have you beaten your donkey these three times? I have come here to oppose you because your path is a reckless one before me. The donkey saw me and turned away from me these three times. If it had not turned away, I would certainly have killed you by now, but I would have spared it.'

Balaam was a prophet. He was also not an Israelite. Three times he was offered money by King Balak to curse the Israelites as Moses led them towards the Promised Land. Twice he refused and sent the messengers back. The third time he left with King Balak's emissaries, telling God that he would bless rather than curse the Israelites. On the way, an angel of the Lord brandishing a sword confronted him. Balaam's donkey saw the angel, but Balaam did not. The donkey was sensitive to the presence of the angel and wanted to warn his master of the danger that lay ahead. Balaam, however, did not stop to wonder why the donkey was behaving as he did, but hurried him on.

Animals are attentive and alert, often more aware than humans of things that are happening around them. Dogs will bark if an intruder is near. Caged canaries used to be kept in coal mines to give the miners early warning of dangerous gas leaks that they could not detect until it was too late. It is easy to think that we look after animals, when, in fact, there are many occasions when they look after us.

Reflection and prayer
Think about the ways in which animals can care for us
and give thanks to God.

BOB MAYO

A dog's faith

Jesus... went to the vicinity of Tyre. He entered a house and did not want anyone to know it; yet he could not keep his presence secret... A woman whose little daughter was possessed by an impure spirit came and fell at his feet. The woman was a Greek, born in Syrian Phoenicia. She begged Jesus to drive the demon out of her daughter. 'First let the children eat all they want,' he told her, 'for it is not right to take the children's bread and toss it to the dogs.' 'Lord,' she replied, 'even the dogs under the table eat the children's crumbs.' Then he told her, 'For such a reply, you may go; the demon has left your daughter.' She went home and found her child lying on the bed, and the demon gone.

In this passage, Mark uses the image of a dog to explain a life of faith. Jesus does not immediately heal the daughter of the Syro-Phoenician woman. He tells her that his mission is to first save the people of Israel.

Desperate to help her child, the woman uses the example of a dog to explain to Jesus what she wants from him. In Jesus' culture, dogs were more likely to have been helpers or guards than family pets, although, in this passage, they are shown to be a part of domestic life. As the family members eat their meal, the dogs sitting under the table look for crumbs to fall.

The woman uses the idea of these dogs under the table as an image of patience and alertness. She tells Jesus that just as a hungry dog waits, in the hope and expectation of falling crumbs of food, so she is waiting for Jesus to act. The dog is both deferential and hopeful, and so is she. Jesus rewards her for her faith and heals her daughter, as she had hoped he would.

Reflection

What does this image of the hungry, patient dog teach us about our own life of faith? How can we be patient about things that we cannot immediately solve while still having faith in God and being ready for when change does happen?

BOB MAYO

Prophecy fulfilled

As they approached Jerusalem and came to Bethphage on the Mount of Olives, Jesus sent two disciples, saying to them, 'Go to the village ahead of you, and at once you will find a donkey tied there, with her colt by her. Untie them and bring them to me. If anyone says anything to you, say that the Lord needs them, and he will send them right away.' This took place to fulfil what was spoken through the prophet: 'Say to Daughter Zion, "See, your king comes to you, gentle and riding on a donkey, and on a colt, the foal of a donkey."'

It is easy to think of animals as bit-part players in a human drama as the story between God and humanity unfolds. Traditional Christian thought was heavily humancentric—animals were only considered in relation to human beings, not in and of themselves. In the Gospels, however, animals play a number of important roles as the narrative unfolds.

The context for our passage is Zechariah 9:9, in which the prophet speaks of a future king presenting himself to Jerusalem while riding on a humble donkey, rather than a majestic horse. It is from the donkey that the disciples learn about the true nature of Jesus' messiahship. They might not have understood at the time that his choice of a donkey was a fulfilment of prophecy, but, looking back afterwards at events leading up to his death and resurrection, they would have remembered these details and realised Jesus' entry into Jerusalem on a donkey had been foretold by the prophets thousands of years before.

In Fyodor Dostoyevsky's 1860s novel *The Idiot*, the hero, Prince Myshkin, talks of being roused from his gloomy state by the bray of an ass: 'I'd never seen one before and I understood at once what a useful creature it was—industrious, strong, patient, cheap, long-suffering. And so, through the ass… my melancholy passed completely.'

The donkey is an animal that it is easy to take for granted, but remember another key role it played (according to tradition), bearing Mary and her unborn child as they and Joseph travelled to Bethlehem.

Reflection

How do we ensure that if people ask for our help, we will be conscientious and reliable—like donkeys!—in how we respond?

BOB MAYO

At the beginning and the end

In the centre, round the throne, were four living creatures, and they were covered with eyes, in front and behind. The first living creature was like a lion, the second was like an ox, the third had a face like a man, the fourth was like a flying eagle. Each of the four living creatures had six wings and was covered with eyes all round, even under its wings. Day and night they never stop saying: '"Holy, holy, holy is the Lord God Almighty," who was, and is, and is to come.'

These four living creatures, seen in a vision by John while on the island of Patmos, were understood by the fathers of the early church to be the four writers of the Gospels. The lion was Matthew because Matthew's Gospel focuses attention on the royalty of Christ, which is the nature of the lion. The ox was Mark because that Gospel emphasises the servant nature of Christ, which is the characteristic of the ox as a beast of burden. The man was Luke because Luke highlights human characteristics in Jesus, while the eagle was John because John pictures Jesus as the divine word, soaring high over all.

Some have seen the four creatures as representing creation—the lion standing for wild animals, the ox tamed animals, the man humans and the eagle birds. In verse 6, the creatures are said to be 'covered with eyes, in front and behind', which suggests that they are alert and knowledgeable; nothing escapes their notice, as the eyes denote ceaseless activity.

These verses show that living creatures appear at both the beginning and end of scripture. There were animals in Genesis, as God created the world. There were also animals in Revelation, as John, who had been imprisoned by the Romans and banished to Patmos, tried to make sense of all that had happened to him. So, animals are embedded in the Old Testament as a part of God's creation and appear in the New Testament as a part of God's revelation.

Reflection

When we care for animals, we are learning how to be responsible for creation and faithful to God.

BOB MAYO

Peace and purity

The next day John saw Jesus coming towards him and said, 'Look, the Lamb of God, who takes away the sin of the world! This is the one I meant when I said, "A man who comes after me has surpassed me because he was before me." I myself did not know him, but the reason I came baptising with water was that he might be revealed to Israel.' Then John gave this testimony: 'I saw the Spirit come down from heaven as a dove and remain on him. And I myself did not know him, but the one who sent me to baptise with water told me, "The man on whom you see the Spirit come down and remain is the one who will baptise with the Holy Spirit." I have seen and I testify that this is God's Chosen One.'

Living creatures abound in John's description here of Jesus as the Lamb of God and the Holy Spirit coming down from heaven at his baptism in the form of a dove.

The figures of the lamb and the dove were rich in significance for the Jewish people. The dove is an emblem of peace; a lamb a symbol of innocence and purity. Of course, Noah sent a dove after the flood to see whether or not the water had begun to recede (Genesis 8:8–11). The dove came back with an olive branch in its beak and that became an enduring symbol of peace that is still used today.

Lambs were used as sacrifices at Passover, the central Jewish festival marking the liberation of the people of Israel from Egypt. These Passover lambs were forerunners of Christ, who was the consummate Passover Lamb (1 Corinthians 5:7), crucified on the Passover. The sacrifice of the Passover lambs marked redemption from slavery in Egypt; Jesus' crucifixion marked the salvation of the world.

Reflection

The dove with the olive branch and the Passover lamb both symbolise God's forgiveness and reconciliation. This work was then taken on by Christ. How do we show the gentleness of the lamb and the peace of the dove in the way that we relate to others?

BOB MAYO

Care for the vulnerable

The Lord wraps himself in light as with a garment; he stretches out the heavens like a tent... He makes springs pour water into the ravines; it flows between the mountains. They give water to all the beasts of the field; the wild donkeys quench their thirst. The birds of the sky nest by the waters; they sing among the branches. He waters the mountains from his upper chambers; the land is satisfied by the fruit of his work. He makes grass grow for the cattle, and plants for people to cultivate—bringing forth food from the earth.

Animals are a part of the originally created world order and they are also our partners in looking after the creation, playing their role in the eco-system of our planet. We should always remember that animals were not put on earth simply to serve the needs of humanity but also to share with us in the wonders of God's world. We need to learn to share that world with them because this can teach us about sharing the world with other people.

Francis of Assisi is said to have taught that people who would exclude any of God's creatures from the shelter of compassion and pity would deal likewise with other people. Jesus showed that this was the case when he challenged the Pharisees' behaviour and attitudes to others on the basis of how they would treat an animal in their care. He asked them, 'If one of you has a child or an ox that falls into a well on the Sabbath day, will you not immediately pull it out?' (Luke 14:5). The Pharisees had nothing to say because they realised the trap that he had set them. If they claimed to keep the letter of the Law (which forbade healing on the sabbath, v. 2), they would be righteous, but unmerciful.

Jesus brought a new world order, which called for mercy and not sacrifice (Matthew 9:13) and the way we treat animals is part of establishing this new way of living.

Reflection

A test of discipleship is how we behave towards those who are weaker and more vulnerable than ourselves. Let us also bear this in mind in our treatment of animals.

BOB MAYO

Covenant creatures

In that day I will make a covenant for them with the beasts of the field, the birds in the sky and the creatures that move along the ground. Bow and sword and battle I will abolish from the land, so that all may lie down in safety… Let them praise the name of the Lord, for at his command they were created, and he established them for ever and ever—he issued a decree that will never pass away. Praise the Lord from the earth, you great sea creatures and all ocean depths, lightning and hail, snow and clouds, stormy winds that do his bidding, you mountains and all hills, fruit trees and all cedars, wild animals and all cattle, small creatures and flying birds.

If our thinking as Christians is too much centred on humanity, to the exclusion of all other living things, we will tend to talk far more often about the covenant that God made with Abraham or Moses than that which God made with the animals. Our verses from Hosea remind us that God did indeed make a covenant with animals as well as humans! This means that we should see animals as sentient beings in their own right, our partners in creation, not simply add-ons to how we want to live our lives. Living creatures are in the world to share the joy of God's creation rather than simply here to serve our needs.

Today, the prime contact that most people in the industrialised world have with animals will be either with those living in a zoo or else with their own pets at home. An appreciation of God's covenant with animals helps us to understand that, while we may be stewards and trustees, we are not the sovereigns of God's creation. The fact that God made a separate covenant with animals means that we have an obligation to share the planet with them and ensure their 'voices' are heard. God created all things and holds all things together, both in heaven and on earth, both visible and invisible (Colossians 1:16).

Reflection

What can we learn from animals about how to care
for God's created order?

BOB MAYO

49

Song of Songs

'Let him lead me to the banquet hall, and let his banner over me be love… If one were to give all the wealth of one's house for love, it would be utterly scorned' (Song of Songs 2:4; 8:7b, NIV).

'This dark, loving knowledge, which is faith, serves as a means for the divine union in this life' (St John of the Cross, The Dark Night of the Soul, Book 2, Chapter 24).

'Prayer is… nothing else than an intimate sharing between friends' (Teresa of Avila).

The Song of Songs (also known as the Song of Solomon) belongs to the part of the Bible known as Wisdom literature, along with Proverbs, Ecclesiastes, Job, Esther, Ruth and Psalms. The book of Jonah also shows signs of the Wisdom literature writers, who balance the texts of the prophets and the Law with a refreshingly pragmatic approach and a more inclusive view of religion, laying emphasis on a good life lived with integrity as pleasing to God.

The Song of Songs uninhibitedly celebrates sexual love. It is rampant with hormones! During the years when all sex was regarded with distaste and suspicion in the church, virginity and celibacy were upheld as the aspirational norms of virtue. As a result, the Song of Songs presented something of a problem. Mysticism offered a resolution—the cheerful sexuality of the book becoming acceptable when it was seen as metaphorical, an inspired expression of the love between Christ and his bride, the church. Thus, it came to be an important text for the great mystics of the Middle Ages, including Teresa of Avila and St John of the Cross, whose feast day we celebrate in the course of this fortnight.

For us, the Song of Songs is redolent with the riches of both physical and spiritual love; the joy of conjugal union and the ecstasy found by the faithful soul in communion with the living God in Christ.

O beloved Mystery, may your Holy Spirit be imprinted indelibly into my being; like a seal placed over my heart or set upon my arm, may all my love and all my strength be dedicated to your glory and your love divine. Amen

Penelope Wilcock

Signs

We rejoice and delight in you; we will praise your love more than wine... Tell me, you whom I love, where you graze your flock and where you rest your sheep at midday. Why should I be like a veiled woman beside the flocks of your friends? If you do not know, most beautiful of women, follow the tracks of the sheep and graze your young goats by the tents of the shepherds.

The Song of Songs is a kind of dramatic poem, its cast consisting of a young woman and a young man deeply in love, overflowing with the erotic anticipation of the consummation of marriage, and a group of friends whose role is the same as the chorus in traditional Greek drama, offering commentary as the story unfolds. In literary terms, this is a sign of the Hellenistic influence on the Bible's Wisdom literature.

Searching for the beloved is a theme that emerges strongly in the Song of Songs. In our passage for today, the maiden appeals to her friends for help in her search for the beloved. They direct her attention to the tracks made by his flock as the way that will surely lead her to him.

In our own searching and seeking, spurred by the restlessness of our soul's hunger for fulfilment, we turn to wise friends who may know the way. Perhaps, therefore, the sheep tracks could symbolise two things for us. They may represent the path trodden by the family of faith—if we follow in the tracks of his flock, staying close to those whose daily walk is with the Shepherd, surely we will find our way to him. Second, a sheep track is a faint path made only by the sheep's passing feet, not a three-lane motorway. If we keep to the way of lowliness and humble simplicity, we will discover him there.

Prayer

O best beloved, my heart's longing, the hope of my soul—when will I find you? Dearest Friend, sometimes you feel so near, other days I almost feel I imagined you. Direct my feet in the paths your flock follow; lead me in your living way; keep me close to you. Amen

PENELOPE WILCOCK

Adoration

Like an apple tree among the trees of the forest is my beloved among the young men. I delight to sit in his shade, and his fruit is sweet to my taste. Let him lead me to the banquet hall, and let his banner over me be love... Listen! My beloved! Look! Here he comes, leaping across the mountains, bounding over the hills.

I wonder if it is a help to us or an impediment that Jesus was a young man. It is possible to get mysticism and eroticism confused—to sublimate unfulfilled passions and desires of human sexuality in religious fervour.

As we draw close to Jesus in adoration, loving him and allowing ourselves to receive his healing, transforming love, we have the chance to pay attention instead to his vision of compassion that has space for all, not based on looks or what the world deems attractive.

Folk traditions include tales and ballads of a young hero who is so gentle and courteous that he is willing to take the hideous and ancient hag for his bride, only to find her transformed on their wedding night, discovering a beautiful princess in his arms.

In seeking the Beloved, it helps to acquire the habit of noticing the distinction between real spiritual principles and what just boils down to aesthetics. Churchmanship, building and music styles, preferences about vestments and décor—these are permissible, as the expression of craftsmanship, order and beauty is worthwhile, but if we rely on them as our path to the presence of the Beloved, we will be disappointed and find they are false trails.

It is the gentleness of loving kindness, the way of understanding and compassion, that will bring us to where Jesus is. This is what it means to 'let his banner over me be love' (v. 4).

Prayer

O dearest Jesus, draw me into the bliss of your presence. As I think of you, the young man sitting at the lakeside, walking the hills of Galilee, how beautiful you are! Help me also to draw close to you in the ordinary everyday—in the tedious encounters, the clumsiness of the unlovely. Help me to find you and touch you. Work your miracle; bring love to life in me.

PENELOPE WILCOCK

Invitation

Look! There he stands behind our wall, gazing through the windows, peering through the lattice. My beloved spoke and said to me, 'Arise, my darling, my beautiful one, come with me. See! The winter is past; the rains are over and gone. Flowers appear on the earth; the season of singing has come, the cooing of doves is heard in our land… Arise, come, my darling; my beautiful one, come with me.'

In 1917, D.H. Lawrence wrote a collection of poems called *Look! We have come through!*, exploring the theme of love achieved after a long time of struggle. Something of the same feeling arises from this rejoicing over the winter and rains ending, the earth in bloom and (wonderful phrase) 'the season of singing' having come.

In England, this would be the month of May, when the bluebells are in flower and the woods ring with birdsong as the sun comes up. Excitement, hope and new beginnings radiate from the above passage. Look! We have come through! The wondrous explosion of life in the season of singing is, of course, connected with regeneration—it is the time of courtship, pairing and birth: 'Arise, come, my darling' (v. 13).

The message of hope in the Christian gospel is also an invitation to new life: 'If anyone is in Christ, the new creation has come; the old has gone, the new is here!' writes Paul (2 Corinthians 5:17), and, 'Behold! I make all things new,' proclaims Jesus in John's vision on Patmos (Revelation 21:5, KJV).

When we remember our human failings in the light of Jesus' grace, thankfulness for our salvation fills us, but here, there is a hint of something more. It is that Jesus not only stoops to rescue us but also woos us, delights in us, loves us most ardently.

'My darling… come with me' (v. 10) is God's invitation to you today, full of happiness and hope. In the words of the traditional Nootka song from the Pacific North West of North America, 'You whose day it is, get out your rainbow colours and make it beautiful!'

Prayer

Jesus, lover of my soul, thank you for choosing me, inviting me. This day will be blessed because I will be living it with you. Amen

PENELOPE WILCOCK

Searching

All night long on my bed I looked for the one my heart loves; I looked for him but did not find him. I will get up now and go about the city, through its streets and squares; I will search for the one my heart loves. So I looked for him but did not find him... I found the one my heart loves. I held him and would not let him go.

I wonder if anything has given you sleepless nights. Have you longed for and looked for something, but never found it? Where is your heart still restless? What are the areas of frustration and lack of fulfilment in your life? Tomorrow will be the feast day of Teresa of Avila. On this eve of her commemoration, we remember that she urged us to keep company with God lavishly—to talk to him, listen to him, really get to know him, as a close friend.

Would you like to make this quiet time as you read these notes—even, maybe, this whole day—an opportunity to spend time with God, talking to him quite frankly about the unfulfilled longings of your heart? Is there still an aching bruise from broken dreams? Tell him about it. Is there a stubborn hope that refuses to die, but seems likely never to come to fruition? Talk to him about it.

Our Bible passage tells a story of yearning, but it has three stages:

- The sleepless night—the time of agonising and longing
- The arising—putting some action into it, going out there and hunting it down
- The finding—the heart's desire realised, love found, a dream come true.

All right, it is an old cliché, but is it still true, that, with God, all things are possible. Who knows, the longing of your heart may be God's Spirit stirring in your soul, the beginning of something wonderful.

Prayer

My Master, my Brother, my Friend, I bring you my dreams, my heart's desire, trusting you with these little seeds of hope. Breathe your Spirit into me. Show me the way to walk in, so that I may be fully alive—the person you meant me to be. Amen

PENELOPE WILCOCK

Ecstasy

Who is this coming up from the wilderness like a column of smoke, perfumed with myrrh and incense made from all the spices of the merchant? Look! It is Solomon's carriage, escorted by sixty warriors, the noblest of Israel, all of them wearing the sword, all experienced in battle, each with his sword at his side, prepared for the terrors of the night.

The charismatic 16th-century Spanish nun Teresa of Avila reformed the Carmelite Order. A born leader, Teresa combined practicality, shrewdness and humour with the visionary ecstasy of mysticism. She said that, 'prayer is nothing else than being on terms of friendship with God' and, to this day, Carmelites follow her example, entering the divine presence with the openness and informality of sitting down with a beloved friend.

She experienced ecstatic union with God in the contemplative prayer that characterised her life and inspired St John of the Cross at a time when, greatly disillusioned, he was on the brink of leaving the order. His participation in her visionary reform movement came at great cost as the religious authorities from which he had broken away imprisoned him in a tiny cell, beating him and semi-starving him.

St John's mystic verse is counted among the greatest treasures of Spanish poetry. His foremost works are *The Dark Night of the Soul* and *Spiritual Canticle*, which is, in effect, a paraphrase in Spanish of the Song of Songs at a time when translation of the Bible into one's own language was forbidden. He spoke of the soul having a secret stairway to heaven, an inner place of private communion with the living God: 'The soul goes by a very secret ladder, which is living faith.'

'Trust God that you are exactly where you are meant to be,' said Teresa of Avila.

Prayer

O precious Jesus, so join my heart to yours that I, too, may be on fire with love for you. May my life be hidden in yours and yours in mine. May my ways and my words reveal your beauty in the ordinary circumstances of my days. For your love's sake. Amen

Penelope Wilcock

SONG OF SONGS 4:1B–2A, 5–6 (NIV)

Vitality

Your eyes behind your veil are doves. Your hair is like a flock of goats descending from the hills of Gilead. Your teeth are like a flock of sheep just shorn, coming up from the washing... Your breasts are like two fawns, like twin fawns of a gazelle that browse among the lilies. Until the day breaks and the shadows flee, I will go to the mountain of myrrh and to the hill of incense.

Who could read the Song of Songs without being impressed and moved by its vitality? It is teeming with life. In this extract, not only is the beautiful woman herself alive, but the imagery chosen—for her eyes, hair, teeth, breasts—is of animals, as though every single bit of her has a life of its own. The writer has a vividly effective way of communicating her quality of vivacity, strength and youth—her sheer animal vitality.

Back in the second century, Irenaeus said, 'Gloria Dei est vivens homo', which means, 'The glory of God is a human being fully alive.' Reading the intense and powerful Song of Songs extolling the intensity of being ignited by love, we could be forgiven for feeling only half alive by comparison.

Such heady experiences are uncommon except in sexual love, yet mystics such as St John of the Cross fasten eagerly on this book of scripture because they can testify to a similar intensity of experience found in prayer, in falling in love with Jesus, that also floods souls with delight, illuminating drab lives with a technicolour vision of wonder.

Is this experience only for lovers and mystics or can anything akin to it be attained by you and me, in the everyday? I believe it can. Of course, we grow staid and middle-aged; our physical exuberance dims and can be compromised as we grow old. Permanent hyper-excitement is unrealistic, even unwelcome—it would wear us out—but we can have the steady glow of faith, the inner upwelling of God's Holy Spirit, a fountain of life that is most deeply satisfying and there for us every day.

Prayer

Holy Spirit of God, saturate my being until I am enlivened by your power and love. May your light and truth burn brightly in my heart. Amen

PENELOPE WILCOCK

Exhilaration

You are a garden locked up, my sister, my bride; you are a spring enclosed, a sealed fountain. Your plants are an orchard of pomegranates with choice fruits, with henna and nard, nard and saffron, calamus and cinnamon, with every kind of incense tree, with myrrh and aloes and all the finest spices. You are a garden fountain, a well of flowing water streaming down from Lebanon.

Due to a lifetime's interest in health matters, I've stored up many nuggets of information for future reference, and I've read about the association between depression and the immune system: they are connected. It is common knowledge that high-quality nutrition, rest, exercise and appropriate hygiene all strengthen or protect our immunity to illness, but some have suggested that wellness is also encouraged by laughter and exhilaration. Exhilaration wakens up the senses, strengthens our sense of aliveness and lifts our mood, enhancing well-being and health.

Our passage for today overflows with flavour and fragrance—aromatic oils and spices, pure water. These are the epitome of health and well-being. The idea of fragrance being beneficial to health is reminiscent of the nosegays carried in medieval times to ward off the plague, and it was found that those who worked with essential oils did indeed see some measure of protection against sickness.

The writer directs our attention beyond this, however, mentioning that this cornucopia of health is locked up inside the beloved, as though the very soul of her is sweet to smell and taste.

Choice fruits and spices, essential oils and pure water all build our health; so does the experience of exhilaration. There is also an inner experience that is elusive to describe—sometimes spoken of as 'the fragrance of Jesus', the presence of his joy in the hidden garden of the soul. This is *shalom*, health, life—the power to transform our inner world regardless of circumstances and transcending physical experience.

Prayer

Creator God, source of all life, make me wise in making healthy choices for my daily life. Come in your healing power to the innermost courts of my heart, bringing hope, the shalom of your life-giving presence. Amen

PENELOPE WILCOCK

Poetry

[She] Awake, north wind, and come, south wind! Blow on my garden, that its fragrance may spread everywhere. Let my beloved come into his garden and taste its choice fruits. [He] I have come into my garden, my sister, my bride; I have gathered my myrrh with my spice. I have eaten my honeycomb and my honey; I have drunk my wine and my milk.

Poetry and fiction have a great advantage over non-fictional prose—they can present great and powerful truths in the viewfinder of the imagination. I wonder how the Song of Songs would read if it were written as an essay or an article for a scientific paper. What would this heady, erotic adventure of being swept off one's feet with wild love boil down to? A discussion of hormones and total collapse of ego boundaries? A documentation of primary and secondary sexual characteristics and their relative function?

In his novel *The Voyage of the Dawn Treader*, C.S. Lewis gives us this wonderful dialogue between the boy Eustace and a star who appears in human form. Eustace tells the star how, 'in our world… a star is a huge ball of flaming gas'. The star replies, 'Even in your world, my son, that is not what a star is, but only what it is made of.' There are some realities that depend on poetry and fiction to do them justice.

The poetry of the Song of Songs not only brings to life for us the sensual delights of love but also its intensity and passion. The language of metaphor and imagination also illuminate the story with the richness and immensity of the Spirit. Its poetry opens up possibilities of a wider understanding—the soul seeking the courts of the King, yearning for union with the Beloved, extolling the delights of spiritual rapture. Poetry and prayer share a common language, and faith relies on imagination to find its reality.

Prayer

O Holy Spirit, who came in tongues of flame at Pentecost, thank you for the life and variety of language, and especially for the wonderful gift of poetry, that builds a glorious chariot to convey the love of the human heart and love divine. Amen

PENELOPE WILCOCK

Ardour

I slept but my heart was awake. Listen! My beloved is knocking: 'Open to me, my sister, my darling, my dove, my flawless one. My head is drenched with dew, my hair with the dampness of the night.'... My beloved thrust his hand through the latch-opening; my heart began to pound for him. I arose to open for my beloved, and my hands dripped with myrrh, my fingers with flowing myrrh, on the handles of the bolt.

Two testimonies evoked the same response in me. One was from someone reporting on a mission meeting the previous night: 'The Lord was really working for us!' The second was someone giving an account of his faith journey: 'God is such a big part of my life now.' In both cases, I reflected that the people concerned hadn't really understood it yet.

Being in love, whether with God or another human being, is a matter of ardour—passion. It takes you over. Crucially, it is bigger than you are. It is not working for you, you're working for it. It is not a part of your life, big or little, but a flame consuming your whole life, waking and sleeping.

Today's passage puts it like this: 'my heart began to pound for him' (v. 4). This love has overwhelmed her physical processes, it's woken her up: 'I slept but my heart was awake' (v. 2).

The Song of Songs celebrates new love—falling in love. Over time, inevitably, lovers settle down. As Isaiah 40:31 (KJV) says, 'They that wait upon the Lord shall renew their strength; they shall mount up with wings as eagles; they shall run, and not be weary; and they shall walk, and not faint.' The first excitement has the power of a soaring eagle, but, as time goes on, the passion persists but steadies from soaring to running. Even with the passing years, however, it does not collapse completely, but just keeps trucking—this ardour, this passion, this love; it walks and does not faint.

Prayer

Give me, majestic Lord, such a vision of your beauty, wonder and grace, that my heart soars up to meet you like an eagle, and I fall in love with you for evermore. Amen

PENELOPE WILCOCK

SONG OF SONGS 5:10–14 (NIV)

Beauty

My beloved is radiant and ruddy, outstanding among ten thousand. His head is purest gold; his hair is wavy and black as a raven. His eyes are like doves by the water streams, washed in milk, mounted like jewels. His cheeks are like beds of spice yielding perfume. His lips are like lilies dripping with myrrh. His arms are rods of gold set with topaz. His body is like polished ivory decorated with lapis lazuli.

In her novel *Northanger Abbey*, Jane Austen—being delightfully shrewd —describes one of her characters thus: '… to a precision the most charming young man in the world. Any further definition of his merits must be unnecessary; the most charming young man in the world is instantly before the imagination of us all.' Another way of putting it would be the old adage, 'Beauty is in the eye of the beholder.'

The young woman of the Song of Songs sees her beloved as 'outstanding among ten thousand' and extols his physical perfection in the most lavish terms.

Theologian Frederick Buechner observed that one person could say that Susie Smith has fallen arches and another that she walks in beauty like the night and both could be speaking the truth equally. Love sees beauty where indifference sees only the mundane.

Because of this, we should not misunderstand the Song of Songs to be about Miss World and Mr Universe—the Ken and Barbie of the Bible, a couple of extraordinary physical perfection—but about how the beloved appears in the lover's eyes.

The insight added by mysticism is that we, for all our ordinariness, are, likewise, cherished by God, who, astonishing though it is to us, sees that we are beautiful because he looks on us with eyes of tenderest love. The opportunity of the love story of faith is the chance to become what the heart of God sees in us.

Prayer

O Lord, fairest of the fair, we worship you in the beauty of holiness, we adore you in your wonder and your grace. Thank you for the comfort and healing and transforming confidence you have given us in your love.

PENELOPE WILCOCK

Friends

> Where has your beloved gone, most beautiful of women? Which way
> did your beloved turn, that we may look for him with you?... Who is
> this that appears like the dawn, fair as the moon, bright as the sun,
> majestic as the stars in procession?... Come back, come back, O
> Shulammite; come back, come back, that we may gaze on you!

The Song of Songs concerns two lovers, but alongside them are also the
friends, who comment and question, offering encouragement. In
today's passage, we see these friends in action. They do not seem that
helpful in the first extract, asking the young woman where the beloved
has gone so that they can look for him with her! In the second extract,
they come across as dazzled admirers. In the third, they seem irritat-
ingly clingy. Hmm.

What about your friends? In this time of reflection, sit quietly with
God—your most intimate and trustworthy friend—honestly reviewing
with him your personal relationships. Who is on board? Have you a
good balance of give and take?

All relationships, to flourish, require mutuality, nourishing both parties. Are there any frankly toxic associations that call for healing or
severance? Can you identify friends whose sanity and wisdom you can
trust, those whose character is noble and example beautiful, those who
will help you to persevere, share your vision and hold the light for you
when your own is dim?

What about your family? Your fellow Christians, colleagues and
neighbours? Can you identify true friends among them? Can you safely
be unguarded and open with them? What kind of a friend are you?

There are no right or wrong conclusions to these questions. Answer-
ing them may lead to further reflection. As friendships significantly
develop our character, however, we do well to seek God's counsel on
this occasionally—asking him, if need be, for a new friend.

Prayer

*Jesus, Friend and Brother, may I walk with my hand in yours all through
this day. By your grace may I be a good friend to others. In your mercy,
send me wise and faithful friends to share my pilgrimage with me. Amen*

PENELOPE WILCOCK

Sex

[He] Your stature is like that of the palm, and your breasts like clusters of fruit. I said, 'I will climb the palm tree; I will take hold of its fruit.' May your breasts be like clusters of grapes on the vine, the fragrance of your breath like apples, and your mouth like the best wine. [She] May the wine go straight to my beloved, flowing gently over lips and teeth.

Sex has ever been a fraught area in church circles. Provided it is channelled uneventfully—in abiding marriage blessed with healthy children—it is celebrated with much joy. Every family with even one member who is divorced, homosexual, transgender or even asexual, however, will know how the church that seemed so welcoming and hospitable can quickly become a cold and inhospitable place.

In the 21st century, the stakes are even higher. In former times, a child born out of wedlock or a marriage that failed could result in excruciating shame and absolute rejection by one's family. In our day, some have escalated differing views on homosexuality to the decisive issue of Christian belief—above even such matters of core belief as theology of the incarnation, the atonement or the Eucharist.

These internal wars have drowned the whisper of Christ's prayer—'That all of them may be one, Father, as you are in me and I am in you' (John 17:21). The strife that has occurred has been so intense that the suicides, alienation and ruined lives it has occasioned have seemed immaterial. How did we let this happen?

Our passage puts godly sex back into context. It was meant for faithfulness, tenderness, ecstasy, pleasure and delight, not power plays or religious politics. May we remember that the way of the gospel is a discipline of love, not law, and two quintessential characteristics of love are respect and gentleness. As the psalmist wrote, 'You make known to me the path of life; in your presence there is fullness of joy; at your right hand are pleasures forevermore' (Psalm 16:11, ESV).

Prayer

O Christ, grant us compassion in our treatment of others and give us grace to channel our own passions into the service of health and peace. Amen

PENELOPE WILCOCK

Nature

Come, my beloved, let us go to the countryside, let us spend the night in the villages. Let us go early to the vineyards to see if the vines have budded, if their blossoms have opened, and if the pomegranates are in bloom—there I will give you my love. The mandrakes send out their fragrance, and at our door is every delicacy, both new and old, that I have stored up for you, my beloved.

I wonder how much of your life is spent outdoors. I wonder how much of your day is taken up with living things and how much with manufactured objects—computers and furniture, tools and machines.

The sense of exuberant life resonating through the Song of Songs arises from its sustained celebration of the natural world—fruits and flowers, domestic flocks and wild creatures. Andrew Marvell's 17th-century poem 'The Garden' shares something of this sense of the intense aliveness of nature:

> *The luscious clusters of the vine*
> *Upon my mouth do crush their wine;*
> *The nectarine and curious peach*
> *Into my hands themselves do reach.*

Marvell encourages us to imagine the ripe and delicious fruit as actually proactive, pressing itself on the human being wandering in the garden—creation as an eager and willing gift! He conjures for us a world in which we have an actual relationship with nature—it is not merely passively ornamental and useful but also alive in the fullest sense.

Countless numbers of people find health, peace and a sense of connection with God's presence in woodlands and gardens, in the hills and by the sea. Spending time in nature is important for our soul's health. Try, if you can, to spend a little while in the fresh air today and smell a crushed leaf, watch a cloud sail by, listen to a bird sing.

Prayer

Creator God, we trace your artistry in the wonder of creation. May we never take this beautiful earth for granted, but do what we can for the safety and well-being of every living thing. Amen

PENELOPE WILCOCK

SONG OF SONGS 8:5B–7 (NIV, ABRIDGED)

Silence

Under the apple tree I roused you; there your mother conceived you... Place me like a seal over your heart, like a seal on your arm; for love is as strong as death, its jealousy unyielding as the grave. It burns like blazing fire, like a mighty flame. Many waters cannot quench love; rivers cannot sweep it away. If one were to give all the wealth of one's house for love, it would be utterly scorned.

If someone asked you the question, 'What is the Bible about?' I wonder what you would say. My guess is that most people would opt for 'God' or 'humanity's search for God'. Either way, 'God' would be somewhere in the answer, which would be entirely correct. The Song of Songs, however, although right there in the Bible, does not mention God. I find that intriguing.

Generally, when critics discuss the Song of Songs, some say that it is not meant to be about God as such, but its inclusion as one of the sacred books of the Bible is to show that human love, including sexual love, is blessed and hallowed by God. Others say that God is in the Song of Songs, but is represented allegorically: the story's bridegroom prefigures Christ and represents God who loves us. As no one really knows, you and I will have to make up our own minds.

In thinking about it, I face another question: 'What is my life about?' I hope this receives the same answer as my first question—God.

It was Francis of Assisi who is reputed to have said, 'Preach the Gospel at all times, and when necessary use words.' Sometimes the occasion calls for me to preach the gospel like Paul did—straight up, no messing, telling it like it is. At other times, it is right to preach the gospel like the Song of Songs—reflecting on the beauty and fragrance of my life, the ardour of my love, my passions, my imagination and my full-blooded humanity—because, in all of that, God is there.

Reflection

Fill Thou my life, O Lord my God, in every part with praise. That my whole being may proclaim Thy being and Thy ways.

From 'Fill Thou my life', by Horatius Bonar, 1866
PENELOPE WILCOCK

Paul's hymns

Early on in his apostolic ministry, Paul took to writing letters and, wonderfully for us, many of his letters have been preserved and served to inspire millions of Christians the world over.

His letters tell us much about his character, as well as his passion for Christ, his love for the people to whom he was writing and his deep yearning that they would learn more about the faith and apply it in their lives day by day.

Experts have pored over his words and, among many interesting literary features, they have discovered that, from time to time, there are changes in his writing style that have suggestions of poetry and song and look very much like something that would have been said or sung corporately. In a world where few could read, there was much to be gained by gathering important truths into memorable songs and sayings. Thus, we can detect in Paul's writings some early hymns. It is hard to say whether he was the author or he picked them up from local congregations and slotted them into his writings. Of course, there will always be debates, too, about which passages are hymns and which are not.

In the coming days, we will have a look at some of the passages that many believe are early hymns recorded by Paul. We know that he was keen on singing—for example, his voice could be heard at midnight, ringing out of the jail in Philippi where he had been imprisoned with Silas (Acts 16:25), which suggests that it came naturally to him to sing hymns, even at what some would consider antisocial hours! His letters also encourage the Ephesians and the Colossians to sing psalms, hymns and spiritual songs (Ephesians 5:19; Colossians 3:16). The early church was a singing church and the glimpses we have of their early hymns tell us that they loved to worship God in song. In this way, they could proclaim together true sayings about God, as well as acknowledge his wonders and mysteries.

As we reflect on these hymns over the next eleven days, may our hearts be drawn into the wonder, love and praise that first inspired their writing.

Michael Mitton

The story in a nutshell

I hope to come to you soon, but I am writing these instructions to you so that, if I am delayed, you may know how one ought to behave in the household of God, which is the church of the living God, the pillar and bulwark of the truth. Without any doubt, the mystery of our religion is great: He was revealed in flesh, vindicated in spirit, seen by angels, proclaimed among Gentiles, believed in throughout the world, taken up in glory.

It is the second part of today's passage that is reckoned to be an early hymn—one that contained a creed in seven brief statements, which could be learned easily by young Christians, who would then have a succinct account of the gospel story.

As we might expect, it begins with the incarnation. Then there is a reference to the work of the Spirit, probably his role in the resurrection (see Romans 1:4; 8:11). This vital activity of the Holy Spirit in the earthly life of Jesus and his resurrection was important to the members of the early Christian community, for they experienced the life of the Spirit, who made real the message and work of Jesus.

Then we have a perhaps unexpected reference to angels. This may be to the angels who witnessed the resurrection (Matthew 28:2), but whatever the exact truth is, it links Jesus with the whole realm of heaven, where angels are in such evidence. Following, there is a reference to the Gentiles and the whole world. The early Christians celebrated the fact that God's love was now breaking out far and wide and extended to those who were once despised. The final piece of this hymn ends with a reference to the ascension. The story begins in heaven and ends in heaven and is all about the coming together of heaven and earth.

This is the story of Christianity in a nutshell. You might think that much has been left out, but sometimes it is no bad thing to identify the core elements of our faith and then draw them deep into our souls, so that they can rise up as a hymn to our Lord.

Reflection

*Try writing a version of a simple declaration of your faith,
then speak or sing it out.*

Michael Mitton

Going down

Let the same mind be in you that was in Christ Jesus, who, though he was in the form of God, did not regard equality with God as something to be exploited, but emptied himself, taking the form of a slave, being born in human likeness. And being found in human form, he humbled himself and became obedient to the point of death—even death on a cross.

The 'Philippian hymn', as it is sometimes called, is reckoned by some to be one of Paul's finest pieces of writing. The context for this beautiful passage is his appeal for the Philippians to live in unity and, for Paul, the greatest inspiration for this is to look at the life of Jesus.

Human nature in Paul's day was little different from how it is now and one aspect of that nature is an ambition to 'get to the top'. Those who are seen to influence the world are those with fame and fortune.

There were celebrities in Paul's day, just as there are in ours. Good fortune made you a success in the eyes of the world, while bad fortune meant the reverse. The early readers of this hymn, therefore, must have read with astonishment that the God whom Paul was commending actually *chose* to go right to the bottom of the heap, which, then, meant being a slave, the lowest of the low.

We know how the hymn continues, but let us pause today and reflect on Jesus' humility.

We gain much comfort from the fact that Jesus came 'down to our level' and so the hymn is very comforting in that sense. The uncomfortable part, however, is that Paul commends the Philippians to have the same attitude as Christ. Our problem is that we can easily think of 'humbling ourselves' in terms of humiliation and becoming a doormat, which is far from what Paul was getting at. True humility, following the example of Jesus, is a genuine and joyful letting go of the need to gain value from prominence. Jesus could accept his status as a slave because he knew he was beloved and had no need to impress anyone.

Reflection

What does 'having the attitude of Christ' mean for you today?

MICHAEL MITTON

Going up

Therefore God also highly exalted him and gave him the name that is above every name, so that at the name of Jesus every knee should bend, in heaven and on earth and under the earth, and every tongue should confess that Jesus Christ is Lord, to the glory of God the Father.

This is one of the great 'therefore's of the Bible.

As with all 'therefore's, what comes next can only happen because of what has come before. In this case, it is clear that God can only exalt Jesus precisely because Jesus has humbled himself as a slave in this world.

It is a most curious 'therefore', too. In normal circumstances, to say 'he chose to become a slave' would be followed by, 'therefore he lived a life of poverty and suffering to the end', but this Philippian hymn declares so beautifully that the kingdom of God is a topsy-turvy kingdom where the last shall be first, the enemy is loved and the meek inherit the earth. Jesus chose to become a slave and, therefore, God has exalted him. Such servant attitudes can cope with exaltation.

Moreover, Jesus does not change his nature in his exalting. The servant heart is so instilled in him that it is not eradicated by being exalted. The Christ who is Lord is still the one who serves and is humble in heart. The person who is exalted by God retains a servant heart and, therefore, any prominence he or she may have will be for the good of all, not as a gain for that person.

The hymn makes clear that we serve a Lord with a supremely humble heart, but it also carries a message to each of us, that Jesus has set us an example and it is an example we are called to follow. Should the Lord call us into any kind of prominence, his expectation is that we will be like Jesus. Whether it be in the home, local church, place of work or politics, it is the servant leaders who often display natural authority and inspire the people around them to flourish.

Prayer

Lord, work in me the mind of Christ and teach me to be content whether I am humbled or exalted.

MICHAEL MITTON

The fullness of God in Christ

He is the image of the invisible God, the firstborn of all creation; for in him all things in heaven and on earth were created, things visible and invisible, whether thrones or dominions or rulers or powers—all things have been created through him and for him. He himself is before all things, and in him all things hold together. He is the head of the body, the church; he is the beginning, the firstborn from the dead, so that he might come to have first place in everything. For in him all the fullness of God was pleased to dwell, and through him God was pleased to reconcile to himself all things, whether on earth or in heaven, by making peace through the blood of his cross.

This is another immense hymn of Paul's about Christ. He wants the Christians at Colossae to have a firm grasp of orthodox belief, because there has been an outbreak of the heresy known as Gnosticism, one that plagued the early church.

Part of the Gnostic belief was that spirit was essentially good and matter evil, which is an idea that many people have fallen prey to. Furthermore, the Gnostics claimed that Jesus was only one among many intermediaries between God and humanity and he was only a partial revelation of God. You can imagine Paul steaming with indignation at that thought as he composed his letter!

He launches in with this wonderful statement about the nature of Christ. It would have been packed with meaning for those battling the Gnostic heresy, but parts of it may feel more obscure to us today.

Try reading this passage out loud and listen to the tone of it. You can hear a great sense of authority in it and, perhaps more than anything else, you will hear the word 'all' many times. You cannot get to the end of this passage and conclude that Jesus was just an inspiring teacher! He is a servant leader who has a loving interest in all things and all people and is devoted to bringing them all together.

Prayer

Read the passage again, replacing 'you' with 'he', so it becomes a hymn of praise to Jesus. Feel your spirit rise!

Michael Mitton

A hymn of enduring hope

Therefore I endure everything for the sake of the elect, so that they may also obtain the salvation that is in Christ Jesus, with eternal glory. The saying is sure: If we have died with him, we will also live with him; if we endure, we will also reign with him; if we deny him, he will also deny us; if we are faithless, he remains faithful—for he cannot deny himself.

The second part of today's passage is a very brief and simple hymn, yet full of comfort and challenge, written by Paul as he was serving his second term of imprisonment, this time during the persecution by Nero. Most people reckon that Paul was never released from this prison and he was facing the very real possibility of death. Endurance, therefore, had become a key theme for his life. Could he maintain his vibrant faith, locked away in a prison cell and facing the prospect of execution? The answer was that he most certainly could, and he was, in fact, very much alive because the life of Christ flowed so deeply in him.

Maybe this brief hymn had a tune to it that Paul sang in the dark hours of night, deeply convinced that there was nothing to fear in death—he would die with Christ and therefore would rise with him. His enduring faith would ensure that he would reign with Christ.

There is a challenge in the hymn, which is that denying Christ cuts us off from him. It ends, however, with the assurance that, even if in the end our faith fails, Christ will be faithful to us. The hymn must have given those early Christians such strength. It reminds me of the poem 'No Coward Soul is Mine' by Emily Brontë that begins:

No coward soul is mine
No trembler in the world's storm-troubled sphere
I see Heaven's glories shine
And Faith shines equal, arming me from Fear

To draw close to Christ brings us in touch with heaven and, when we contact its glory, we are armed sufficiently to see off fear.

Prayer
Lord, when I am imprisoned by fear, shine the light of heaven into my soul.

Michael Mitton

Part of the family

> Blessed be the God and Father of our Lord Jesus Christ, who has blessed us in Christ with every spiritual blessing in the heavenly places, just as he chose us in Christ before the foundation of the world to be holy and blameless before him in love. He destined us for adoption as his children through Jesus Christ, according to the good pleasure of his will, to the praise of his glorious grace that he freely bestowed on us in the Beloved.

Traditionally, Ephesians is ascribed to Paul and we shall spend the next three days with its opening paragraph.

In the Greek original, verses 3–14 are one sentence. It is a doxology and you get the sense it was written by Paul not so much after hours of careful thought and study, but more as an eruption of praise and delight that flows from his grateful heart.

The main theme of this song of praise is an acknowledgement of how much Christ has done for us and how this affects our identity in this world. So, at the start, Paul declares that we are the recipients of every spiritual blessing. Remember, he was in prison when he wrote this and could have felt very far from being blessed, but his eyes take him beyond the immediate to the 'heavenly places'.

He then moves on to the theme of our adoption. The adoption process in the Roman world was a very thorough one, at the end of which the adopted child was viewed as being a completely new person. Paul includes a note here that the Father has chosen to adopt us because he has delighted in us. In verse 6, he uses a word for us that is also used in Luke 1:28, where Mary is described as 'highly favoured'.

My mother was adopted at the age of two, having lived in a children's home previously. She never lost the sense of delight at being chosen and taken into a home and given a new family. It is this delight that Paul is touching on. He feels it and it shapes how he lives in this world. If we draw this truth into our hearts, it is truly transformative.

Prayer

Father, thank you for choosing me.

Michael Mitton

The healing of divisions

In him we have redemption through his blood, the forgiveness of our trespasses, according to the riches of his grace that he lavished on us. With all wisdom and insight he has made known to us the mystery of his will, according to his good pleasure that he set forth in Christ, as a plan for the fullness of time, to gather up all things in him, things in heaven and things on earth.

Paul was writing to a people who, whether they were Jews or Greeks, lived in dread of God's disapproval. All religions had complicated systems, usually involving sacrifices, for steering negative divine judgement away from their lives. People were very aware of their sins and the penalties for sins. The message of grace, therefore, was such a wonderful relief—that life was not about anxiously trying to impress God so he would withdraw his punishments, but, rather, about being utterly loved by God who delighted to forgive wrongdoings and had provided the means for us to live as free people. At last, we need not be divided from God.

Paul delights not only in this but also in the fact that this same God now invites us into his council chambers, so to speak, and talks to us about his plans for this world. The master plan is sensational: it is to rid the world of all the divisions that have caused such terrible destruction—family divisions, tribal divisions, gender divisions, social divisions, all the divisions that we see all too clearly around us today. The plan, in Christ, is that all things are to be gathered up in him. It is he who is able to bring together the things of heaven with the things of earth—and therein lies our hope.

As we look on our painfully divided world, we need to take hold of this passage and ask God to show us how we can be part of his plans to gather up all things in Christ.

Reflection

Take some time to think about what is divided in your immediate world, then enter the courts of God as his adopted child and listen to him.

MICHAEL MITTON

A surprise inheritance

In Christ we have also obtained an inheritance, having been destined according to the purpose of him who accomplishes all things according to his counsel and will, so that we, who were the first to set our hope on Christ, might live for the praise of his glory. In him you also, when you had heard the word of truth, the gospel of your salvation, and had believed in him, were marked with the seal of the promised Holy Spirit; this is the pledge of our inheritance towards redemption as God's own people, to the praise of his glory.

So we come to the final part of this doxology and here Paul gives a clear example of the breaking down of divisions. The 'we' in verse 11 refers to the Jews, the 'you' in verse 13 are the Gentiles, but, in verse 14, he refers to 'our' inheritance. So, the two groups are now one, indicating that 'God's own people' (v. 14) is made up of the different, once divided groups, coming together through the work of grace.

We get an interesting insight into Paul's understanding of the Spirit when he refers to him as the 'pledge' or 'our inheritance' (v. 14). The Greek word *arrabon* is full of significance. It is a word from the business world and means something like a deposit, but more than that because it also serves as a guarantee that the full amount will be paid. The arrabon, therefore, is an assurance that the full amount is on its way. So, the *arrabon* of the Spirit is part of that which we will receive fully in heaven. This means that we can have every reason to look with excitement to our eternal future. It also means something of that eternal future is breaking in on us now. The Spirit brings the gifts of heaven to our earth now and this is all part of our inheritance. No wonder Paul got so excited in that prison cell all those years ago!

Prayer

Blessed be my Father, who, through Christ has adopted me as his child, shares with me his plans and who, through the gift of the Spirit, releases heaven's life into our world. Alleluia!

MICHAEL MITTON

EPHESIANS 5:11–15 (NRSV)

Time to wake up!

Take no part in the unfruitful works of darkness, but instead expose them. For it is shameful even to mention what such people do secretly; but everything exposed by the light becomes visible, for everything that becomes visible is light. Therefore it says, 'Sleeper, awake! Rise from the dead, and Christ will shine on you.' Be careful then how you live, not as unwise people but as wise.

Today's hymn—'Sleeper, awake...' (v. 14)—is our briefest one. It is probably a fragment of an early Christian hymn that may have been used at baptisms. You can imagine people singing it rousingly as the candidate emerged dripping and smiling from the water, celebrating his or her new resurrection life.

Paul uses these lines of a hymn in the midst of his exhortation for people to avoid the works of darkness and live in the light. He is concerned for those believers who have made a profession of faith, but have been drawn into a lifestyle that is far from Christian. It is as if they are drifting into a dark world where, spiritually speaking, they are falling asleep and, indeed, in one sense, dying. So, Paul uses this hymn as a kind of alarm clock to wake them up and bring them back to life. Maybe it had a stirring tune that the first readers would hear in their minds. It may have taken them back to the life-giving moment of their baptisms.

As we journey on in the life of faith, it is not difficult to find our faith waning and we, too, can wander into a twilight world where we start compromising our Christian values simply because we have become spiritually dozy and accommodated ourselves to the world around us. If we suspect this, then it is no bad thing to go back to this simple hymn fragment and let it resonate in our soul. The hymn carries a wonderful promise—if we show our intention to rise up, then Christ will be there to shine his light on us and we will come back to full life.

Reflection

As you reflect on your life, is there any part that needs to hear the wake-up call of Christ?

MICHAEL MITTON

The goodness of God

But when the goodness and loving-kindness of God our Saviour appeared, he saved us, not because of any works of righteousness that we had done, but according to his mercy, through the water of rebirth and renewal by the Holy Spirit. This Spirit he poured out on us richly through Jesus Christ our Saviour, so that, having been justified by his grace, we might become heirs according to the hope of eternal life.

Titus was in Crete when Paul wrote to him and later tradition has it that he was a bishop there. Paul's letter is full of practical leadership advice for Titus, who is having to build a church in a community known for its disreputable behaviour (see 1:12). There is much, therefore, in his letter about living a holy lifestyle. Then he drops in today's passage, which many feel could be an early hymn.

It may be that Paul was aware he was giving Titus a kind of Christian behaviour handbook, which was beginning to look somewhat onerous! He wants to be clear that the Christian life is not a life of strenuous battle against our wayward nature, but primarily about fully appreciating what we have been given and living in response to that. So, this hymn is drawing Titus and his Cretan community back to the wonderful truth that the story of Jesus is ultimately a story about the goodness, loving-kindness and mercy of God.

We may feel that we battle against all kinds of influences of darkness in ourselves and in our society, but Paul wants us to remember that the Spirit of God has been poured out on us. These verses are a wonderful hymn about the nature of grace.

There are days when, by watching the news or simply reflecting on our own lives, we can feel fairly depressed. If that is so, then it is worth turning to these verses so that we might feel the pouring of the Spirit on us and become aware of all that we inherit as children of God. Then we can live as messengers of this grace to our world.

Prayer

God, my Saviour, pour your Holy Spirit upon me and fill me with your life.

MICHAEL MITTON

Extravagant love

When I was a child, I spoke like a child, I thought like a child, I reasoned like a child; when I became an adult, I put an end to childish ways. For now we see in a mirror, dimly, but then we will see face to face. Now I know only in part; then I will know fully, even as I have been fully known. And now faith, hope, and love abide, these three; and the greatest of these is love.

The passage 1 Corinthians 13 is often called 'the hymn of love'. Whether it was a hymn or not, we do not know, but we do know that it has become one of the most famous pieces of literature of all time. Paul had clearly come to the conviction that the quality he wanted to see more than anything else in the church was love. This inspired chapter has led countless people into a deeper way of love.

After detailing the qualities of love, Paul ends this hymn with a declaration of the permanency and enduring nature of love. Then he notes that there is a mystery in love: our understanding of it can only be partial in this world. He uses the analogy of a mirror. Corinth was famous for its mirrors, but even its best ones were made of polished metal and the reflection was far from perfect.

So, what is the mystery in love, the bit that is unclear? Maybe it is the whole question of the love of God and suffering? Love does not solve all our problems, but it does help us to live with them. One day we will have an answer to all our questions, but, until then, the task is to love trustingly.

At one level, Jesus made Christianity very simple—it is about loving God and loving people (Matthew 22:37–40). Christians down the ages have been prone to avoiding both these commands! Paul is clear about this, though—the way of love is the way we must follow. The translation given in THE MESSAGE of the last line of the hymn sums it up beautifully: 'Trust steadily in God, hope unswervingly, love extravagantly' (1 Corinthians 13:13).

Reflection

Read the whole of 1 Corinthians 13, asking God to highlight words that are important for you today.

MICHAEL MITTON

Songs of praise: Abide with me

A while ago, I was helping a church organist choose hymns and she was lamenting the fact that so few traditional 'evening hymns' are still sung as part of weekly worship. While many smaller churches no longer hold services of evening prayer because of dwindling numbers, for other, more thriving, congregations 'evening service' means an exuberant knees-up. Of course, the tradition of Evensong is maintained by cathedrals and other centres of choral excellence.

'Abide with me', by the Scottish clergyman Henry Francis Lyte, is perhaps the quintessential evening hymn (rivalling 'The day thou gavest', the 'signature hymn' for the Women's World Day of Prayer), sung most often to the gentle tune 'Eventide', composed by William Henry Monk. 'Abide with me' was written in 1847 and finished as Lyte was in his final weeks of battling tuberculosis. Understandably, then, its tone is somewhat melancholy and so it has been a popular choice for funerals. It also features regularly at Remembrance Day services, major sporting events and is reputed to have been among the numbers played by the band as the *Titanic* sank beneath the waves.

I first came across it in the children's classic *Seven Little Australians* (1894). The vivacious (and, it has to be said, rebellious) Judy, 13, has been fatally injured while rescuing her baby brother during a picnic in the Outback. As night falls and they wait in vain for help, her sister recites verses from 'Abide with me' to provide comfort for the dying girl.

With its emotional—not to say lugubrious—overtones, we may be tempted to dismiss 'Abide with me' as typical of a Victorian tendency to wallow in deathbed pathos. Read the lines as a poem, though, and what soon becomes apparent is their vigour and psalm-like drawing together of scriptural images and concepts. Far from sweetly sentimental or embarrassingly overwrought in its expression of grief, this hymn offers robust hope to sustain those who are enduring times of darkest shadow. It sounds a powerful note of faith in its repeated call for God to 'abide' with us. I trust that the following passages will not only aid reflection in this season of remembrance but also help to commend a well-loved hymn to a new audience.

Naomi Starkey

Linger with us!

And they drew nigh unto the village, whither they went: and he made as though he would have gone further. But they constrained him, saying, Abide with us: for it is toward evening, and the day is far spent. And he went in to tarry with them. And it came to pass, as he sat at meat with them, he took bread, and blessed it, and brake, and gave to them. And their eyes were opened, and they knew him; and he vanished out of their sight.

'Abide with me; fast falls the eventide; the darkness deepens; Lord, with me abide. When other helpers fail and comforts flee, Help of the helpless, O abide with me.'

As noted, we may be used to thinking of this hymn as something funereal or at least written specifically for singing at a tranquil service of evening prayer, so it can be startling to realise that the opening words are pretty much a direct quote from the Emmaus road story. I have written previously about what I sense as a poignancy in Jesus' post-resurrection appearances. Yes, the Lord is risen, wonderfully and beyond his followers' wildest dreams, but, no, things are not the same as before. He is no longer with them as he once was, night and day, walking the paths of Galilee in their company. Now, even as he sits down with two of them to eat and they recognise him, he is gone.

In modern translations, the evocative word 'abide' has been replaced with the more prosaic 'stay'. While it is crucial for Bible versions to be accessible to a wide audience, we should be careful to not lose nuances of language that an older word may convey. 'Abide' includes overtones of 'lingering'—younger generations might even say 'hanging out with'—that I do not think are quite encompassed by 'stay'.

Reflection

Luke uses the same pattern of taking bread, giving thanks, breaking it and sharing it when he describes the Feeding of the Five Thousand (9:16) and the Last Supper (22:19). It is in the Eucharist, the taking and breaking, pouring and blessing, of bread and wine, Jesus' body and blood, that we can meet most intimately with our risen Lord today.

NAOMI STARKEY

Not forgotten

The life of mortals is like grass, they flourish like a flower of the field; the wind blows over it and it is gone, and its place remembers it no more. But from everlasting to everlasting the Lord's love is with those who fear him, and his righteousness with their children's children—with those who keep his covenant and remember to obey his precepts.

'Swift to its close ebbs out life's little day; Earth's joys grow dim; its glories pass away; Change and decay in all around I see; O Thou who changest not, abide with me.'

The longer we live (and in the course of my ministerial duties I have met more than a few centenarians!) we become more aware of the passage of time. Where once birthdays seemed to come round with glacial slowness, now they flash past almost before we can take them in. The psalmist compares a human lifespan to the swift flowering and fading of wild flowers, small flashes of colour that spring up and then disappear forever. Lyte's hymn uses the image of the 'little day'—apt words for this time of year when, in the northern hemisphere, the winter darkness increases by the day.

In the midst of such inescapable change and decay, we badly need the abiding presence of a heavenly Father whose unknowable name, YHWH (Exodus 3:14), hints at eternal being, constant renewal, unstoppable and abundantly creative life. We may feel swamped by change, struggling to stay afloat in a sea of transition and turmoil. Clinging to the strength of our abiding Father, we can be safe and at peace.

This season of remembrance focuses on preserving the memories of those whose lives were cut short in military conflict. As the years pass, memories—like names on a war memorial—inevitably start to fade and individual faces and stories are forgotten. We never forget those who mean most to us, however long ago we may have lost them. So how can we fear that God, who loves us beyond measure, will forget about us?

Reflection

Human forgetting is, in some ways, merciful because memories bring pain as well as joy.

NAOMI STARKEY

Resisting lies

Your enemy the devil prowls around like a roaring lion looking for someone to devour. Resist him, standing firm in the faith… And the God of all grace, who called you to his eternal glory in Christ, after you have suffered a little while, will himself restore you and make you strong, firm and steadfast. To him be the power for ever and ever. Amen

'I need Thy presence every passing hour. What but Thy grace can foil the tempter's power? Who, like Thyself, my guide and stay can be? Through cloud and sunshine, Lord, abide with me.'

Reading about 'roaring lions' brings to mind Christians being thrown to wild beasts in Roman arenas. The Greek word translated 'devil' in English—*diabolos*—had the original meaning of 'slanderer', this being the word chosen to translate the Hebrew 'satan', or 'accuser'.

If we are used to thinking of the devil as a kind of dark lord or medieval horned-and-hooved monster, we should remember that the damage done by malicious talk can be more dangerous than any bluntly evil assault. We may be prepared to resist outright wickedness, but slander can be so sly yet so treacherously undermining of an individual, a community, an institution…

Evil is the antithesis of all that is good, warping our view of the world and ourselves. Once we start seeing ourselves—and others—as more or less than we really are, reality is warped. We can end up being drawn away from the presence of our heavenly Father who made us and loves us and into the distorted perspective of the 'father of lies' (John 8:44, NIV). Then, all manner of evil can flow from that.

Wonderfully, though, both our hymn verse and Bible passage remind us where true power and strength lie, where we can turn in full confidence of healing and restoration. God has called us, and, even if his calling takes us through the hardest of times, we can trust him that he will be faithful to us (1 Thessalonians 5:24).

Reflection

Do we use our words to build up and heal (which may involve challenge, at times) or to further the work of the father of lies?

Naomi Starkey

1 CORINTHIANS 15:52B–57 (KJV)

Death and victory

For the trumpet shall sound, and the dead shall be raised incorruptible, and we shall be changed. For this corruptible must put on incorruption, and this mortal must put on immortality. So when this corruptible shall have put on incorruption, and this mortal shall have put on immortality, then shall be brought to pass the saying that is written, Death is swallowed up in victory. O death, where is thy sting? O grave, where is thy victory? The sting of death is sin; and the strength of sin is the law. But thanks be to God, which giveth us the victory through our Lord Jesus Christ.

'I fear no foe, with Thee at hand to bless; Ills have no weight, and tears no bitterness. Where is death's sting? Where, grave, thy victory? I triumph still, if Thou abide with me.'

Today, the sting of death will feel particularly sharp for those who have lost somebody in military conflict. Those who die thus have so often been very young men (and, increasingly, women), departed in the midst of the years when life and energy should flow, not be stopped. In such a context, invoking concepts of 'victory' and 'triumph' can seem inappropriate, even offensive, but there is a wider perspective here.

The sounding of the trumpet is inextricably linked to the idea of the 'day of the Lord', which recurs throughout scripture (the two quotations above are from Isaiah 25:8 and Hosea 13:14). On that day, God will come decisively to bring deliverance, judgement, salvation and the righting of all wrongs. Death, too, will be finally defeated.

That is far from denying the anguish of bereavement or, indeed, the fearful prospect of death, which loomed for Henry Lyte in his mid-fifties. It is a stirring reminder that we are in the hands of the everlasting Father and he will keep us safe, eternally, no matter what happens to our mortal bodies.

Reflection

'You will not abandon me to the realm of the dead, nor will you let your faithful one see decay. You make known to me the path of life; you will fill me with joy in your presence, with eternal pleasures at your right hand'
(Psalm 16:10–11, NIV).

NAOMI STARKEY

Heaven's morning

'And you, my child, will be called a prophet of the Most High; for you will go on before the Lord to prepare the way for him, to give his people the knowledge of salvation through the forgiveness of their sins, because of the tender mercy of our God, by which the rising sun will come to us from heaven to shine on those living in darkness and in the shadow of death, to guide our feet into the path of peace.'

'Hold Thou Thy cross before my closing eyes; Shine through the gloom and point me to the skies. Heaven's morning breaks, and earth's vain shadows flee; In life, in death, O Lord, abide with me.'

The deathbed imagery is strong here, but, as we have seen, this was an author who was writing from first-hand experience of years of illness, which was now terminal. Despite the 'gloom', 'shadows' and 'closing eyes', the light of heaven shines through, brighter than any earthly radiance. When we experience hard times, lying awake in the smallest, darkest hours of the night and worrying away over our predicament, the first streaks of morning can be a welcome relief. How much more amazing, then, to envisage 'heaven's morning'.

Our Bible passage is from the song of Zechariah, after the miraculous birth of his son, John. It is one of the canticles (known as the Benedictus, from its opening words in Latin: 'Blessed be the Lord God of Israel') used in the service of Morning Prayer, recited or sung after the New Testament reading. It is an exuberant celebration of not only a wonderful baby but also the hope of Messianic promises fulfilled. A great light will indeed shine on those 'living in the land of deep darkness' (Isaiah 9:2, NIV)—a new day will dawn and change everything forever.

Reflection

'The city does not need the sun or the moon to shine on it, for the glory of God gives it light, and the Lamb is its lamp. The nations will walk by its light, and the kings of the earth will bring their splendour into it. On no day will its gates ever be shut, for there will be no night there' (Revelation 21:23–25, NIV).

NAOMI STARKEY

MALACHI 4:1–3 (KJV)

Heaven's healing

For, behold, the day cometh, that shall burn as an oven; and all the proud, yea, and all that do wickedly, shall be stubble: and the day that cometh shall burn them up, saith the Lord of hosts, that it shall leave them neither root nor branch. But unto you that fear my name shall the Sun of righteousness arise with healing in his wings; and ye shall go forth, and grow up as calves of the stall. And ye shall tread down the wicked; for they shall be ashes under the soles of your feet in the day that I shall do this, saith the Lord of hosts.

'Come not in terrors, as the King of kings, But kind and good, with healing in Thy wings; Tears for all woes, a heart for every plea. Come, Friend of sinners, and thus bide with me.'

This verse of 'Abide with me' is one of three not usually included in modern hymnbooks. The striking image in the passage of the 'Sun of righteousness' with 'healing in his wings' (v. 2) could have been inspired by winged sun motifs, as found in the religions of ancient Egypt and Mesopotamia. This is no mere sun god, however, but the 'Lord of hosts', creator of the universe, who will give his people strength to 'tread down the wicked' (v. 1) like so much ash. The sturdy vigour of young calves is promised to those who 'fear' (or, we might say, 'revere') the Lord God (v. 2).

At first glance, hymn and Bible passage seem to be at odds here, the former emphasising kindness, consolation and God as the friend of sinners, the latter exulting in the destruction of the proud and wicked. Surely, though, the defining feature of the 'proud' is that they think they have no need of God's forgiveness and so, tragically, cannot benefit from his healing love? Salvation, forgiveness, redemption—each is a free gift held out to all, but such gifts can either be accepted—and their healing power unleashed—or rejected. If they are rejected, if the proud continue in their defiance and rebellion, then heavenly grace cannot take hold of them.

Prayer

Humble our proud hearts, Lord, until we are ready to heed your quiet words of forgiveness.

NAOMI STARKEY

Abiding still

Abide in me, and I in you. As the branch cannot bear fruit of itself, except it abide in the vine; no more can ye, except ye abide in me. I am the vine, ye are the branches; He that abideth in me, and I in him, the same bringeth forth much fruit: for without me ye can do nothing. If a man abide not in me, he is cast forth as a branch, and is withered; and men gather them, and cast them into the fire, and they are burned. If ye abide in me, and my words abide in you, ye shall ask what ye will, and it shall be done unto you.

To close this series of readings, we turn from the words of Lyte's hymn to the best-known Bible passage about 'abiding'—Jesus' words to his disciples in the Upper Room on the night before his betrayal and death.

The hymn begs God to 'abide' with us; these verses from John's Gospel remind us that we, too, have a part to play. The way of fruitfulness, fullness of life, is found by grafting ourselves so closely into the Son of God that we become one with him. Without the inexhaustible energy of God flowing into us and through us, we will eventually dry up and wither away.

How do we graft ourselves in this way? By giving ourselves to worship, fellowship with other Christians, sharing the Eucharist, immersing ourselves in the study of scripture and, above all, committing ourselves to prayer. Astonishingly, the promise here—the promise of Jesus himself—is that if we become thus sufficiently aligned with the will of our Heavenly Father, we will be so transformed, we will no longer want to seek anything contrary to his purposes. We will then truly be able to 'ask what [we] will' (v. 7) and be confident that we will receive it. It is a breathtaking promise, an awesome privilege, a daunting challenge!

Reflection

'If ye keep my commandments, ye shall abide in my love; even as I have kept my Father's commandments, and abide in his love' (John 15:10).

NAOMI STARKEY

My favourite scriptures

It feels slightly self-indulgent to be writing about favourite Bible passages—almost as if the life of faith were only about delight and we were all like children in a sweetshop, picking out the most appealing treats. There is a serious and more creditable point to this, however.

The following Bible passages are some of those that strike me most. They speak to me clearly about God and his grace. God loves me, as he loves each of us, whom he has created. If we let him, he will guide us. He has inspired the authors of these Bible verses, and you and me, reaching out to each of us and offering himself. So, these words are one example of the way in which God plants the seed of love in our hearts, drawing each of us towards himself. As Augustine famously wrote, our hearts are restless until they rest in him.

The passages that I have chosen show the ways in which God gets through and makes sense to me. It is not that I am special in some way, but I am sure these examples might well speak powerfully to others, too.

It was not hard to choose which parts of the Bible to refer to—we all know of verses that appeal to us more than others. There is also that phenomenon, which happens in a lesser form with any good literature, of a few words leaping off the page at you so that you think suddenly, 'Wow!' They pack a powerful punch, so that your mind races, considering the possibilities of, 'My grace is sufficient' (2 Corinthians 12:9) or 'Blessed are those who mourn' (Matthew 5:4), for example. They do not have to be grand emotional declarations. Indeed, often it can be the quieter thoughts that prompt us to ponder and roll them around in our head most. This is surely the work of the Holy Spirit within us, prompting 'sighs too deep for words' (Romans 8:26).

So, the following Bible passages leapt out at me—a couple of psalms, some of Jesus' words in the Gospels and some parts of the epistles. All are direct and powerful, telling me what God is like and drawing me into his heart.

Rachel Boulding

Light for my path

The Lord is my light and my salvation; whom then shall I fear: the Lord is the strength of my life; of whom then shall I be afraid?... For in the time of trouble he shall hide me in his tabernacle: yea, in the secret place of his dwelling shall he hide me, and set me up upon a rock of stone... I should utterly have fainted: but that I believe verily to see the goodness of the Lord in the land of the living.

We see by God's light. Without him, we would be stumbling in darkness. It is only by his light that we are able to grasp and to do anything. We need his light to show us the way; we rely utterly on him.

How does this work for each of us, day by day? For me, it means that I need God's light from the moment I wake up. Just as I need some sort of light so that I can see to get out of bed and get dressed, I have to have God's light to do anything. I am completely dependent on him, like a tiny baby is dependent on someone to look after him or her.

The Lord is also my salvation. He has saved me from the snares of selfishness and all the other traps the world sets. It is not that I am wonderfully good (far from it!), but God is always showing me another way and a better choice. He calls me back—usually fairly gently—from the worst excess and the dangerous paths.

So, God might remind me—by a word in scripture or some completely unexpected place—of ways in which I could reach out to others and share his love. He might plant the idea of writing to a troubled or ill friend or just sending a quick card. Every single day, he draws me back from my less appealing self and towards his better ways.

Reflection

Consider one little thing that you can do in the next 24 hours that God's light might be guiding you towards. It might seem like an insignificant gesture, but it might mean a great deal to someone, especially when done with wholehearted love.

RACHEL BOULDING

What am I afraid of?

The Lord is the strength of my life; of whom then shall I be afraid?
When the wicked, even mine enemies and my foes, came upon
me to eat up my flesh, they stumbled and fell... My heart hath
talked of thee, Seek ye my face: Thy face, Lord, will I seek... Thou
hast been my succour: leave me not, neither forsake me, O God
of my salvation. When my father and my mother forsake me, the
Lord taketh me up.

What am I afraid of, I sometimes wonder? It is easy to become mired in
fear—from niggling worries, to anxieties about the family or even large-
scale foreboding about the future of society—but this psalm reminds
me that I should not be afraid. As usual in Psalms, the fears are personi-
fied, so it reads, 'Of whom then shall I be afraid?' (v. 1) rather than 'Of
what'.

Sometimes, when we focus our fears on people rather than unspeci-
fied abstract entities, they can shrink. I always find it is the nameless
dread that has most power. If, instead, I try to isolate just what is getting
to me, it seems much smaller. When I had breast cancer, for example, I
found it helpful to work out exactly what was bothering me. I asked
myself, 'What would be so bad about dying sooner rather than later?' I
would be surrounded by loving family and friends, cared for physically
and I would be placing myself in God's loving embrace. So it wouldn't
be too tough on me, but it would be very hard on my family. I would
be afraid for them. Having niggled away at all this, I could then try to
work out ways, however small, to make the situation easier for those
around me—and for myself.

This psalm reminds me that I need not fear. Terrible things might
well happen—and they do—but it gives me a glimpse of the way that
God 'taketh me up' (v. 12) and enfolds me in his love.

Reflection

*'The Lord is our clothing, wrapping us for love, embracing and enclosing
us for tender love, so that he can never leave us, being himself everything
that is good for us.'*

Julian of Norwich
RACHEL BOULDING

Ultimate intimacy

O Lord, thou hast searched me out and known me... For lo, there is not a word in my tongue: but thou, O Lord, knowest it altogether. Thou hast fashioned me behind and before: and laid thine hand upon me... For my reins are thine: thou hast covered me in my mother's womb. I will give thanks unto thee, for I am fearfully and wonderfully made: marvellous are thy works, and that my soul knoweth right well. My bones are not hid from thee: though I be made secretly, and fashioned beneath in the earth. Thine eyes did see my substance, yet being unperfect: and in thy book were all my members written.

Here is another psalm, one that is not just my favourite, but a favourite of many. Like Psalm 27, it speaks of the closeness of God and his fighting for us, his being absolutely on our side when we face our enemies. In Psalm 139, it is the ultimate intimacy that strikes me: God knows each one of us better than we do ourselves. I may be a confused, inconsistent jumble of mixed motives and contradictions, but God has somehow sorted through the muddle and found someone to love. This is true of every single one of us, however difficult we might be.

Even if we feel we are unwanted—even if we are unwanted, if we have been abandoned or rejected or betrayed by parents, one-time friends, beloved wives or husbands or anyone else—we are never completely unloved. God still, always, loves us.

People can be so cruel, but God will never leave us. When I think of those I know who have been let down in devastating ways by those closest to them—wives who have thrown out their husbands like rubbish, husbands who have treated their wives like flimsy dolls and all the other gross selfishness that many of us are capable of—then I do feel angry. I know, however, that God still loves both parties, and me. All of us are sinners in need of forgiveness.

Prayer

Dear Lord and Father, forgive me for all my self-indulgences and spiritual pride. Help me to remember that you know me better than anyone, yet still you love me. Amen

RACHEL BOULDING

Lead me in your ways

Such knowledge is too wonderful and excellent for me: I cannot attain unto it. Whither shall I go then from thy Spirit: or whither shall I go then from thy presence?... Yea, the darkness is no darkness with thee, but the night is as clear as the day: the darkness and light to thee are both alike... Try me, O God, and seek the ground of my heart: prove me, and examine my thoughts. Look well if there be any way of wickedness in me: and lead me in the way everlasting.

Today's verses suggest a way forward from the fears and twistedness we looked at yesterday. God knows us thoroughly, in all our tangled ways, but he draws us out of these, towards his glorious light: our darkness is not dark to him (v. 11). We cannot escape from God (v. 6)—his is the love that will not let us go. This is the God who searches for us, as Francis Thompson describes so vividly in 'The Hound of Heaven':

> *I fled Him, down the nights and down the days...*
> *I fled Him, down the labyrinthine ways*
> *Of my own mind.*

Sometimes, we can only wonder, amazed, at God's perseverance, but, gradually, we can make other responses, too. Wonder will always be part of our relationship with God, just as part of our own private prayer can always be adoration. This can take its place alongside determined seeking of the Lord in other actions.

So, in practice, by beginning our days with a time of prayer, we can offer our praise to God and ask him to examine our thoughts. Following the pattern of verses 23–24, we can lead on from God's loving and gentle probing of us to his drawing us into his ways. If we align ourselves to God like this, every day, he will put in our minds his ways for us to follow; opportunities and words will pop up.

Prayer

And we most humbly beseech thee, O heavenly Father, so to assist us with thy grace, that we may continue in that holy fellowship, and do all such good works as thou hast prepared for us to walk in...

Prayer after Holy Communion, BCP
RACHEL BOULDING

Right now, turning to God

Therefore take no thought, saying, What shall we eat? or, What shall we drink? or, Wherewithal shall we be clothed? (For after all these things do the Gentiles seek) for your heavenly Father knoweth that ye have need of all these things. But seek ye first the kingdom of God, and his righteousness; and all these things shall be added unto you. Take therefore no thought for the morrow: for the morrow shall take thought for the things of itself. Sufficient unto the day is the evil thereof.

Here, we seem to have gone back to the fears of Psalm 27. God keeps having to tell us to not be afraid, throughout the Bible.

This is not the debilitating, nameless dread of what might happen, however, but the practical anxiety about how we keep body and soul together. We know that many people rely on food banks and charity shops for the basics, not the extras, and this is in rich countries, never mind the poorer places, where people die every day of poverty. Should we be shocked by the way Jesus dares to say this?

Surely Jesus is talking about the worries themselves, not the actual business of food and clothing. It is our attitude that he is tackling, not the nuts and bolts of our housekeeping. As he does elsewhere, when talking about camels going through the eyes of needles and other extreme figures of speech, he is deliberately exaggerating to make a point about where our priorities should lie. Right now, today, we need to seek God.

This is surely one of the gifts of the mindfulness movement, which encourages a focus on the present moment. In its current iteration, it draws on a number of faith traditions, but on solidly Christian ones, too—though this is not always admitted by those who might want to make it sound exotic. It can be practised with integrity by Christians, especially as it encourages us to acknowledge the presence of God in each moment. Others might think that there is only the moment to be mindful of, but some of us will find God there.

Reflection

Think of one worry that is distracting you from God. Right now, can you turn away from it and towards him?

RACHEL BOULDING

The Father longs to give gifts

Ask, and it shall be given you; seek, and ye shall find; knock, and it shall be opened unto you: for every one that asketh receiveth; and he that seeketh findeth; and to him that knocketh it shall be opened... If ye then, being evil, know how to give good gifts unto your children, how much more shall your Father which is in heaven give good things to them that ask him?

What is stopping me from applying these promises to my situation, now? I know that the times I have done this—asked God for something in a straightforward way—he has given it, blessing me richly. OK, I have asked for a fresh way of praying, for example, rather than for extra height or a cash windfall. Often it has not turned out quite as I had expected...

Perhaps the question is, yet again, what am I afraid of? Perhaps I am worried that God will not consider me or my request worthy, but it is perfectly all right so long as we do not ask things of God as if he were a slot machine or a capricious tyrant—he is our loving Father and knows our needs before we do.

Prayer is a matter of reminding ourselves that we are in his presence and opening ourselves to his grace. It never seems to be a case of asking for things such as good looks or worldly success, as if from a shopping list. When we are praying for other people, especially if they are ill or troubled, we are simply bringing them before God, commending them to him. He knows the details of their needs better than we do.

Prayer is something like a process of me becoming more aware of God's ways, but I still need to know that God is longing to bless me. The image of him standing at the door and knocking is surely right (Revelation 3:20). I need to open up to him each day and, in that wonderful give and take of any loving relationship, he will help me to do this.

Prayer

O God, from whom all holy desires, all good counsels, and all just works do proceed; Give unto thy servants that peace which the world cannot give...

Collect for Peace, Evening Prayer, BCP

RACHEL BOULDING

Fail again. Fail better

For this cause I bow my knees unto the Father of our Lord Jesus Christ, of whom the whole family in heaven and earth is named, that he would grant you, according to the riches of his glory, to be strengthened with might by his Spirit in the inner man; that Christ may dwell in your hearts by faith.

These verses tell us more about God's gifts and the way he is keen to pour them into us. This is a prayer for the Christians in Ephesus—something that we do still as we pray for others every day. The writer is asking that Christ 'may dwell in your hearts by faith' (v. 17) and all else flows from this. It is painful to break off in the middle of verse 17, but I want to focus on each part of what the writer is saying here, the better to appreciate the riches of God's glory.

So, what is the writer asking for, what is this inner strength (v. 16) that builds up to Christ living in our hearts? We all want that resilience which enables us to keep going through troubles and pick ourselves up after each of our many failures. After all, it is how we try and fail better afterwards that matters. As the playwright and author Samuel Beckett put it in *Worstward Ho*, 'Ever tried. Ever failed. No matter. Try again. Fail again. Fail better.'

When we pray and, inevitably, our minds wander, what matters most is not that we have strayed, but how we bring ourselves back. There is no use beating ourselves up over the fact that our powers of focus are not perfect—they never will be—so it is what we do in the next moment that matters. That is why we need the inner strength to leave our failures behind and gently bring our attention back to God. As ever, he will help us in this. It is not a matter of striving in our own strength, alone, for he dwells in our hearts. Whether we let him in or not, he will always be there.

Reflection

Think of one failure that has got you down. How might you 'fail better' at it, or something similar, in the future?

RACHEL BOULDING

EPHESIANS 3:17B–21 (KJV)

The more I give, the more I have

That ye, being rooted and grounded in love, may be able to compre-
hend with all saints what is the breadth, and length, and depth, and
height; and to know the love of Christ, which passeth knowledge,
that ye might be filled with all the fulness of God. Now unto him that
is able to do exceeding abundantly above all that we ask or think,
according to the power that worketh in us, unto him be glory in the
church by Christ Jesus throughout all ages, world without end. Amen

This is a stirring evocation of God's glory. The line of thought builds
steadily from the foundation of God's love (v. 17b), through the sheer
amazingness of its scope, to our own share in it, as we are urged 'to
know the love of Christ' (v. 19) and 'be filled with all the fulness of God'
(v. 19). Then there is a response of overflowing gratitude and praise.

These verses trace our relationship with God, beginning with his love
for us, which is beyond anything we can understand, and our reaction
to the gifts that he has given and 'the power that worketh in us' (v. 20).
It is quite a promise, but what does this really mean in my inglorious,
ordinary life?

Yes, it is a source of inspiration. When times are hard, or even just
lacklustre or boring, we can turn to this passage, and others like it, to
remind ourselves of the true picture—the fact that we are rooted in
God's limitless love: this is the basis of our whole life. It is not just that
God is powerful and on our side, though—we are in a relationship with
him. It is the overflowing grace of a love that we are fully part of. We
experience it in a great cycle of giving, receiving and being renewed.
Shakespeare's description of earthly love in *Romeo and Juliet* (Act 2,
Scene 2) is a reflection of it, when Juliet says:

> *My bounty is as boundless as the sea.*
> *My love as deep: the more I give to thee*
> *The more I have, For both are infinite.*

Reflection

*Pause for a good long minute to be amazed at the unending fullness of
God's love.*

RACHEL BOULDING

COLOSSIANS 3:1–5 (NRSV)

In God in our deepest being

So if you have been raised with Christ, seek the things that are above, where Christ is, seated at the right hand of God. Set your minds on things that are above, not on things that are on earth, for you have died, and your life is hidden with Christ in God. When Christ who is your life is revealed, then you also will be revealed with him in glory. Put to death, therefore, whatever in you is earthly: fornication, impurity, passion, evil desire, and greed (which is idolatry).

Developing some of the ideas in yesterday's passage, here the writer talks about our dwelling with God, but takes it in a different direction— a more practical one. Despite our being loved by God and loving him, we are still living in the ordinary world, still swayed by earthly temptations and sins.

If some of these sins might be a bit distant from our regular experience, we can surely think of various others or parallel temptations. It might be a while since some of this 'evil desire' was a problem for us, but is it not rather similar when we do not consider others as real people, with feelings like our own?

How do we turn away from our besetting sins, which gnaw away at us, as we are urged to do here and throughout the Bible? The clue is in the earlier verses of today's passage, in that wonderful phrase, 'your life is hidden with Christ in God' (v. 3). We cannot see it or understand it properly, but we are intertwined with God; we are in him in our deepest being. This is a reality. All those other temptations and twistedness might be horribly powerful for a while, but they are hollow in their essence. Eventually, we might work this out—though some of us are pretty slow at grasping the truth or quick at forgetting it if we do realise it.

We know that it really is God's world and our lives are bound up in his: that is the way he made us and the whole universe.

Prayer

Loving Father, draw me to you to glimpse the myriad ways in which my life is hidden and bound together in yours.

RACHEL BOULDING

Finding an attitude of gratitude

As God's chosen ones, holy and beloved, clothe yourselves with compassion, kindness, humility, meekness, and patience. Bear with one another and, if anyone has a complaint against another, forgive each other; just as the Lord has forgiven you, so you also must forgive. Above all, clothe yourselves with love, which binds everything together in perfect harmony... And whatever you do, in word or deed, do everything in the name of the Lord Jesus, giving thanks to God the Father through him.

Here is an inspiring vision of our life with God—but it is not all simple uplift. A crucial part of the message is about how we should behave. There are practical things we can do. We can have the right basic approach (v. 12), including kindness and patience, as well as acting in the right way (vv. 13, 17), by forgiving others and giving thanks.

Some of us struggle with the meekness and forbearance we are called to show, trying to find a balance between this and being a doormat—especially when working out how to forgive those who have behaved outrageously. We can try, however, recalling this mention of our own forgiveness by God (v. 13) and remembering that we are not the only ones whom God loves. God is the Father of all of us sinners.

Most of us should at least be able to be thankful. We can try to cultivate an attitude of gratitude. This does not have to be false, like the 'Eat your greens—the starving millions would be grateful for that' sort of instruction that we sometimes inflict on children. It is surely more a matter of recalling the amazing facts of what God has done for us and letting them play in our minds, gradually sinking in. As these ideas dance around inside us, what else can we do but rejoice in gratitude? This approach can spill out into all that we do (v. 17).

Prayer

We bless thee for our creation, preservation, and all the blessings of this life; but above all, for thine inestimable love in the redemption of the world by our Lord Jesus Christ; for the means of grace, and for the hope of glory.

A Prayer for the Conditions of Mankind, Morning Prayer, BCP

RACHEL BOULDING

Keeping faith and loving longest

Now faith is the substance of things hoped for, the evidence of things not seen... By faith Abraham, when he was called to go out into a place which he should after receive for an inheritance, obeyed; and he went out, not knowing whither he went... These all died in faith, not having received the promises, but having seen them afar off, and were persuaded of them, and embraced them, and confessed that they were strangers and pilgrims on the earth.

The idea of faith can seem so abstract, I struggle to grasp its meaning, but it is a living thing that is the focus of my life. God has faith in each one of us: it is something that he does first and to which we respond. As with love, our response is a pale reflection of God's gifts to us, which are so full of grace: 'We love him, because he first loved us' (1 John 4:19).

So, faith is something that God does and we follow what he started. God keeps on having faith in us. He does not give up on us, even when we give up on both him and ourselves. As he did with the people of Israel, throughout the Old Testament, God keeps calling us back to his love.

Faith is about believing that God's promises are true—that he sent his Son to save us and he will always care for us—but, more than this, we carry on, even when it appears to make no logical sense. Anne Elliot, the outwardly quiet heroine of *Persuasion* by Jane Austen, speaks poignantly of the 'not very enviable privilege' of 'loving longest, when existence or when hope is gone', obliquely referring to her love for her future husband, when it seems as if it is all over between them. In the novel, her faith is rewarded and our faith in God will also be more than vindicated.

Reflection

These eleven passages are ones that have had an impact on me. Can you pick a favourite that speaks directly to you? Name one aspect of your chosen verses that give them such power. Why do you think this element matters so much to you?

RACHEL BOULDING

Minor prophets

The other day, I saw a well-known poet described as having 'modest talent'. Talk about damning with faint praise! I am glad that the twelve 'minor prophets' never knew they would be called 'minor'. They are so called purely because their writings are shorter than those of the 'major prophets'.

Zephaniah, Haggai, Zechariah and Malachi come from different times in the history of Judah, but all lived when the southern kingdom was having a difficult time (the northern kingdom, Israel, had been conquered long before this). Like the better-known prophets, their words are full of both threat and promise, designed to call the people to more wholehearted service of God and to justice and peace in society. They often write in poetry, which is a way of getting straight to the heart of the matter and to the hearts of their audience. Prophecies would normally have been read out loud, so you might try doing this yourself to feel their full impact.

Not long ago, I wrote this as my Facebook status: 'A prophet is someone who accurately predicts the present.' Yes, these prophets are sometimes eerily accurate in prefiguring Jesus. They also talk a lot about the future 'day of the Lord', a day of both justice and of restoration. The first thing we must look for in reading them, however, is what their words would have meant for their own day.

Their role was to pinpoint the indifference and injustices in their own society, which prevented God's will being done. They were also called to spell out what the consequences would be for their society if things did not change and instil in the people a vision of how much better things could be if they obeyed God. Only when we have grasped this can we tease out the implications for our own society and churches.

Are there 'prophets' in our own society who provide the same challenge and hope? They may not be within the walls of the church, for God calls unexpected people. Perhaps as you read these notes, you can think of those who are speaking out about what is evil or good in our contemporary world.

Veronica Zundel

ZEPHANIAH 1:1–3 (NRSV, ABRIDGED)

This is getting serious

The word of the Lord that came to Zephaniah… in the days of King Josiah son of Amon of Judah. I will utterly sweep away everything from the face of the earth, says the Lord. I will sweep away humans and animals; I will sweep away the birds of the air and the fish of the sea. I will make the wicked stumble. I will cut off humanity from the face of the earth, says the Lord.

Failing to keep promises is a weakness of mine, of which I am ashamed. Jesus told us to not make extravagant pledges, swearing we will do this or that, but here is God apparently failing to keep an age-old promise made to Noah, that the human race would never again be destroyed (Genesis 9:8–11). What is going on?

We should be aware that Zephaniah is speaking at a time when there had been no prophecy for two generations. He is prophesying in an age when the northern kingdom, Israel, had been conquered almost a century before, and the southern kingdom, Judah, was beginning to face a similar fate at the hands of the new superpower, Babylon. Like all the prophets, he attributes this danger to the sins of the people and kings of the nation. Now a new king, Josiah, has begun to make religious reforms, demolishing the shrines to pagan gods and calling people to serve God alone and do justice in God's name.

Into this situation, Zephaniah speaks with passion, predicting suffering for the whole world as a result of Judah's disobedience. His tone may sound exaggerated, yet this is the flip side of God's calling on the Jews to be 'a light to the nations' (Isaiah 49:6). If the light goes out, the whole world suffers. Zephaniah provides, as it were, the prophetic back-up for Josiah's reforms.

All government requires prophetic voices, either to call it to account or affirm its best actions. Power tends to obscure our vision and we need visionaries who are outside the system to warn or encourage our leaders.

Reflection

What is the role of Christians in relation to government today? Is it to seek high office or critique those in power or, perhaps, both?

VERONICA ZUNDEL

It takes two (or three)

Gather together, gather, O shameless nation, before you are driven away like the drifting chaff, before there comes upon you the fierce anger of the Lord, before there comes upon you the day of the Lord's wrath. Seek the Lord, all you humble of the land, who do his commands; seek righteousness, seek humility; perhaps you may be hidden on the day of the Lord's wrath.

Which do you respond to better, threats of punishment or promises of reward? Perhaps each is appropriate at different times. To be safe, Zephaniah offers both, although the reward is rather uncertain: 'perhaps you may be hidden' (v. 3). Being a true disciple does not mean following God simply for the sake of our own advantage, though, does it?

Zephaniah, like every good preacher, offers a way out. The nation, to avert disaster, must seek not just God but also the actions and attitudes that God requires: righteousness (which could also be translated as 'justice') and humility. These are the natural and spiritual antidotes to injustice and pride.

I am intrigued by the opening words: 'Gather together, gather' (v. 1). This seems to suggest that, in order to follow God's ways, especially if we have wandered a long way from them, we need each other. We need to get together, to encourage and challenge each other, learn 'the things that make for peace', as Jesus put it (Luke 19:42). Surely this is the point of belonging to a church—not just to worship on a Sunday but also to disciple each other in love.

It says something, too, about the nature of worship. It is certainly good to praise God together, to plead together to God for ourselves, our neighbours, our enemies and the world, but another prime purpose is to form our attitudes and behaviour into the shape of Jesus. If Sunday worship does not affect Monday to Saturday, it is not really worship at all.

Prayer

'I appeal to you therefore, brothers and sisters, by the mercies of God, to present your bodies as a living sacrifice, holy and acceptable to God, which is your spiritual worship' (Romans 12:1). Pray that you may learn what this means for you.

VERONICA ZUNDEL

Better times are coming

Sing aloud, O daughter Zion; shout, O Israel! Rejoice and exult with all your heart, O daughter Jerusalem! The Lord has taken away the judgments against you, he has turned away your enemies. The king of Israel, the Lord, is in your midst; you shall fear disaster no more… I will deal with all your oppressors at that time. And I will save the lame and gather the outcast, and I will change their shame into praise and renown in all the earth. At that time I will bring you home, at the time when I gather you; for I will make you renowned and praised among all the peoples of the earth, when I restore your fortunes before your eyes, says the Lord.

'Before your eyes' (v. 20) is a phrase we are perhaps more used to coming from the mouths of conjurers or those selling 'miracle' products, but what God promises here is no conjuring trick.

In our second passage from Zephaniah, we encountered 'the day of the Lord' (2:2) as a threat, a day of judgement and destruction, but that was only the 'labour pains' of something much better (see Romans 8:22). Now we learn what the final outcome of 'that day' is to be. It is salvation: the oppressors will be defeated, the lame will run, the outsiders will be included. The vision is not just for 'daughter Zion' (I love that term) but for 'all the earth' (3:14 and 19).

Is this promise just for the end of time or for Zephaniah's own day? It may be both—change now *and* transformation at the end. Often we view salvation as a 'ticket to heaven', to be cashed in when we die. The Old Testament's view is a transformation of everything in time and space, affecting the physical universe—and the New Testament tells us it begins with Jesus.

If 'the kingdom of God' is already happening here and now, there are things we can do to reveal it and further it. God could recreate us and the world without any help from us, but the Bible shows that God wants to work on it together with us.

Prayer

'Sing aloud, O daughter Zion' (v. 14). Sing a favourite song to God as your praise today.

VERONICA ZUNDEL

If you build it, they will come

Then the word of the Lord came by the prophet Haggai, saying: Is it a time for you yourselves to live in your panelled houses, while this house lies in ruins? Now therefore, thus says the Lord of hosts: Consider how you have fared. You have sown much, and harvested little; you eat, but you never have enough; you drink, but you never have your fill; you clothe yourselves, but no one is warm; and you that earn wages earn wages to put them into a bag with holes. Thus says the Lord of hosts: Consider how you have fared. Go up to the hills and bring wood and build the house, so that I may take pleasure in it and be honoured, says the Lord.

Soon after his conversion, Francis of Assisi was praying in a little ruined church when he heard a voice saying, 'Build my church.' Initially he took it to mean that he should rebuild the chapel he was praying in, but, as he gathered others to help, he realised the call was much bigger in its scope—to create a new community of radical Christians who would recall the wider church to its roots of simplicity and service.

The aim of Haggai's call in today's passage seems to be to spur on the people in their unenthusiastic rebuilding of the temple in Jerusalem after the exiles' return from captivity in Babylon, but is this really about repairing a sacred building? Could it ultimately be about restoring the people's faith and trust in God, and calling them to wholehearted service of God? The building is just a symbol of God's presence, a functional place for them to get together and become a community.

My own church has never had its own premises, but we are very much focusing at the moment on how to rebuild our depleted community after some significant losses we could not prevent. This process is not easy, but we remember that numbers attending are not the only measure of growth. The Jewish people grew a great deal in maturity in exile, even though there were few who returned.

Reflection

Can you remember times of 'exile' for you or your church that have become times of spiritual growth?

VERONICA ZUNDEL

A word to the worried

Yet now take courage, O Zerubbabel, says the Lord; take courage, O Joshua, son of Jehozadak, the high priest; take courage, all you people of the land, says the Lord; work, for I am with you, says the Lord of hosts, according to the promise that I made you when you came out of Egypt... For thus says the Lord of hosts: Once again, in a little while, I will shake the heavens and the earth and the sea and the dry land; and I will shake all the nations, so that the treasure of all nations shall come, and I will fill this house with splendour, says the Lord of hosts... The latter splendour of this house shall be greater than the former, says the Lord of hosts; and in this place I will give prosperity, says the Lord of hosts.

Do you sometimes feel, 'I can't do this—it is just too hard'? Sometimes what life or God demands of us just seems impossible. Yet, this is often just where God acts. Zerubbabel, the governor of Judah, and Joshua, the high priest, are overseeing the reconstruction of the temple, but they are losing heart. They need a prophet like Haggai to remind them that, ultimately, this is God's work, not just theirs, and to hold before them a picture of how good things will be when they have finished.

Like other prophets, Haggai has his eye on both the immediate goal —a restored temple—and on the end, when God will restore all things. The point of the people's work is not just to have a rebuilt place of worship but also to help them work for the ultimate renewal of all creation (see Romans 8:21).

Who are the 'prophets' who inspire you to keep going? They may be prominent Christian writers or speakers or friends who have the gift of saying the right thing. As mentioned in the introduction, they may not even be Christians, just public figures who stand for the values of justice and peace. If you can, thank them for their inspiration.

Prayer

If you are despairing of your current situation, turn to God and pour it all out.

VERONICA ZUNDEL

A passionate God

So the angel who talked with me said to me, Proclaim this message: Thus says the Lord of hosts; I am very jealous for Jerusalem and for Zion. And I am extremely angry with the nations that are at ease; for while I was only a little angry, they made the disaster worse. Therefore, thus says the Lord, I have returned to Jerusalem with compassion; my house shall be built in it, says the Lord of hosts, and the measuring line shall be stretched out over Jerusalem. Proclaim further: Thus says the Lord of hosts: My cities shall again overflow with prosperity; the Lord will again comfort Zion and again choose Jerusalem.

Have you ever been in love? Were you jealous when your beloved spent time with other people or activities? Love and jealousy seem to go together for many of us, until we are more secure in our relationship and we trust our partner. Then we can relax and let them go, knowing he or she will come back to us. We have a right to be jealous, though, if the one we love forms an intimate relationship that threatens our own.

The God of jealousy and anger, whom we see here, is very different from the 'impassible' God of traditional theology. We may have been taught that God is beyond emotion and unaffected by our actions, but we see throughout the Old Testament, and in Jesus, that God is passionately involved with people and history. Our sins and our sufferings actually make God upset!

I think we need to see God's anger towards the 'nations that are at ease' (v. 15)—such an evocative phrase—as the anger of parents who see their child being the target of a playground bully. Anger can be the flip side of love. In Hosea 13:8, God's anger against those who oppress God's people is compared to that of 'a bear robbed of her cubs'.

Writing in the early days of the return from exile, Zechariah stirs up the people to show their love for God by rebuilding the temple. What might we need to rebuild in order to show our love?

Reflection
How can we best express to God our own anger at injustice?

VERONICA ZUNDEL

Dressed up

Then he showed me the high priest Joshua standing before the angel of the Lord, and Satan standing at his right hand to accuse him. And the Lord said to Satan, 'The Lord rebuke you, O Satan! The Lord who has chosen Jerusalem rebuke you! Is not this man a brand plucked from the fire?' Now Joshua was dressed in filthy clothes as he stood before the angel. The angel said to those who were standing before him, 'Take off his filthy clothes.' And to him he said, 'See, I have taken your guilt away from you, and I will clothe you in festal apparel.' And I said, 'Let them put a clean turban on his head.' So they put a clean turban on his head and clothed him in the apparel; and the angel of the Lord was standing by.

As a child, John Wesley was the last of his family to be rescued from a house fire. Later, he would refer to himself, using Zechariah's image, as 'a brand plucked from the fire'. It is a powerful picture of rescue and salvation.

In Zechariah's vision, Satan is 'the accuser', which is the main role of this figure in the Old Testament. In the book of Job, for instance, Satan acts as a rather ambivalent servant of God who asks to test Job. He is evil, but under God's control. Here he wants to have a go at the high priest, who is vulnerable among the small number of people back from exile.

God, however, restrains Satan and, instead, chooses to honour Joshua by dressing him in clean clothes, rather like the father in the parable of the prodigal son dresses his pigsty-stained son in the finest robe and a ring. Clothing is, in fact, a central metaphor in the New Testament, particularly in the letters of Paul (see, for instance, 1 Corinthians 12:23; Ephesians 4:24; Colossians 3:12–14). I once wrote a poem in which I portray Christ wearing our dirty, torn clothes, so that he can dress us in his own robe of light, the wearing of which enables us to imitate him.

Reflection

When we accuse or judge our fellow Christians,
are we doing Satan's work?

VERONICA ZUNDEL

God versus religion

Say to all the people of the land and the priests: When you fasted and lamented in the fifth month and in the seventh, for these seventy years, was it for me that you fasted? And when you eat and when you drink, do you not eat and drink only for yourselves?... Thus says the Lord of hosts: Render true judgments, show kindness and mercy to one another; do not oppress the widow, the orphan, the alien, or the poor; and do not devise evil in your hearts against one another.

The more I read the Bible, the more I realise that God is not very interested in religious practices. How else can we interpret verses such as Amos 5:21: 'I hate, I despise your festivals, and I take no delight in your solemn assemblies' or Hosea 6:6: 'For I desire steadfast love and not sacrifice, the knowledge of God rather than burnt offerings'?

Zechariah casts doubts on the religious practices the people of Judah kept up in their exile in Babylon and whether or not they actually showed a desire to serve God at all. Were they just designed to preserve the superficial customs and culture of their nation, while failing to practise what Jesus called the 'weightier matters' of justice and mercy (Matthew 23:23)? Note that Zechariah casts an uncomfortable light on not only the people's fasting but also on their feasting.

Honouring God in our eating and drinking might involve thinking about whom we invite or, indeed, the source of our food and whether or not people (or the land) were exploited in its production.

How would our society measure up in terms of showing kindness and mercy, not oppressing the widow, the orphan, the alien and the poor? I do not think we can call ourselves a 'Christian society' unless we take care of our most vulnerable. Biblical theology has political repercussions and we should not be ashamed of this. Meanwhile, our worship often focuses on individual salvation or a future heaven, but says little about the needs of this existing world, which is God's world. Should we focus less on praising God and more on what God actually wants?

Prayer

Lord, make me an instrument of your peace.

VERONICA ZUNDEL

Chosen to change the world

Thus says the Lord of hosts: Peoples shall yet come, the inhabitants of many cities; the inhabitants of one city shall go to another, saying, 'Come, let us go to entreat the favour of the Lord, and to seek the Lord of hosts; I myself am going.' Many peoples and strong nations shall come to seek the Lord of hosts in Jerusalem, and to entreat the favour of the Lord. Thus says the Lord of hosts: In those days ten men from nations of every language shall take hold of a Jew, grasping his garment and saying, 'Let us go with you, for we have heard that God is with you.'

My Jewish 'honorary aunt' was queuing to see the film *Chosen* (from the book by Chaim Potok), but there were two queues. A man next to her took one look at her and said, 'This is the wrong queue; the chosen are over there'! Whatever you think about the 'chosenness' of the Jewish people, they have certainly made an impact on the world. Jewish involvement in science, the arts, politics, is hugely disproportionate to the tiny number of this people. It does make one wonder if God was involved…

The stirring prophecy in today's passage depicts the whole world catching on to God's people after seeing how their God has blessed them. Can we simply transfer this prophecy to Christians? It is a bit more complicated, for Paul tells us in Romans 9—11 that the Jewish people are still central to the world's salvation. My summary is, 'You don't have to be Jewish to be a Christian, but it helps'!

I like the portrayal of 'relationship evangelism' here: 'Come, let us go… to seek the Lord of hosts; I myself am going' (v. 21). It is only by observing our walk with Jesus that others will be convinced to seek him, but we are not meant to point it out like the Pharisees; if our life really is better, they will notice anyway. As Francis of Assisi is reputed to have said, 'Preach the gospel at all times; use words if you have to.'

Reflection
'Let your light shine before others, so that they may see your good works and give glory to your Father in heaven' (Matthew 5:16)

VERONICA ZUNDEL

War no more

Rejoice greatly, O daughter Zion! Shout aloud, O daughter Jerusalem! Lo, your king comes to you; triumphant and victorious is he, humble and riding on a donkey, on a colt, the foal of a donkey. He will cut off the chariot from Ephraim and the warhorse from Jerusalem; and the battle-bow shall be cut off, and he shall command peace to the nations; his dominion shall be from sea to sea, and from the River to the ends of the earth.

What do people mean when they say they want 'strong leadership'? I suspect it often means a decisive leader who tells them what to think and do and, in political terms, a leader who will stand up to whoever we think our enemies are. This passage offers a very different type of leader.

It is usually, and probably rightly, seen as a picture of Jesus, riding into Jerusalem on a low-grade mount—the equivalent, perhaps, to driving a really old and beaten-up car. It is a picture of humility and gentleness. We do not often focus much on the second verse, however, which depicts him as a prince of peace, the one who ends wars around the world. I find the workaday donkey he rides and the war horses he is going to 'cut off' to be an interesting contrast. What if we substituted 'bicycle' for 'donkey' and 'tank' for 'war horse'?

What this is emphatically not is a portrayal of a military general charging into battle on his highly trained horse or a bomber primed to destroy cities. When Jesus returns, it will be in order to renew the world, not destroy it.

So, is this merely a vision of a future 'peaceable kingdom' or should we be living as though it were already here? My understanding is that, if Jesus is the bringer of peace, we, his disciples, should also be working for peace. Of course, peacemaking starts small, learning to make peace among our fellow believers or in our workplace, but it should not stop there. We need to be peacemakers in the wider world, by actively exploring alternatives to war.

Reflection

Read Psalm 46. Verse 10a can also mean, 'Stop fighting, and know that I am God.'

VERONICA ZUNDEL

Compassion without limits

And I will pour out a spirit of compassion and supplication on the house of David and the inhabitants of Jerusalem, so that, when they look on the one whom they have pierced, they shall mourn for him, as one mourns for an only child, and weep bitterly over him, as one weeps over a firstborn… On that day a fountain shall be opened for the house of David and the inhabitants of Jerusalem, to cleanse them from sin and impurity.

Since the summer of last year, there has been a huge media focus on the centenary of World War I, the war that was supposed to end wars but did not. Quite rightly, we have focused on the men and women who died for what they believed to be a just cause, but what about the men and women they killed and their mothers and wives and husbands and children?

This is another passage that is normally seen as a prophecy about Jesus, the one who was 'pierced' on the cross. What could it have meant to its first audience, who had no clue that the Messiah would have to die? I wonder if this relates more closely to the passage we read yesterday, about the end of war. What if soldiers suddenly began to feel compassion for 'the one… they have pierced' (v. 10), the victim of their violence, who probably has as little real connection with the causes of the war as the one who killed him does? Surely, if 'a spirit of compassion' (v. 10) falls on the 'house of David', they will no longer be able to kill in the name of God?

King David, after all, was not allowed to build God's temple, but was passed over in favour of his son, Solomon, because David was 'a man of blood'. Right from early on in the Bible, there is a strand of thinking that abhors violence as being against the will of God.

I put forward a modest proposal. When we remember the 'glorious dead' of our own country, let us also remember those (including many civilians) whom they killed or maimed. If we did this, would we be so ready to go to war?

Prayer

Pray for any countries or regions that are suffering violent conflict today.

VERONICA ZUNDEL

Giving to God

A son honours his father, and servants their master. If then I am a father, where is the honour due to me? And if I am a master, where is the respect due to me? says the Lord of hosts to you, O priests, who despise my name. You say, 'How have we despised your name?' By offering polluted food on my altar. And you say, 'How have we polluted it?' By thinking that the Lord's table may be despised. When you offer blind animals in sacrifice, is that not wrong? And when you offer those that are lame or sick, is that not wrong? Try presenting that to your governor; will he be pleased with you or show you favour? says the Lord of hosts.

Confession time: have you ever been in urgent need of a present for someone and ended up giving them an unwanted gift that someone else gave you and a card that has lain in your drawer for years? I know I have.

Malachi is focused on what we give God and whether or not we give it in good faith. He is concerned that the priests are sacrificing animals that are impaired or old, so the sacrifice does not diminish the value of the herd. It is not that God actually needs perfect lambs, goats or, indeed, any animal at all (see Psalm 50:9–10). Rather, the people's offerings to God are meant to show their wholehearted commitment to God and God's Law. Instead, they are giving as little as they can get away with, which does not bode well for their daily following of God's righteousness.

What 'sacrifices' does God ask of us and how are we responding? Psalm 51:17 tells us, 'The sacrifice acceptable to God is a broken spirit; a broken and contrite heart, O God, you will not despise.' This does not mean that we are to make ourselves miserable—some of us are miserable enough already! It does mean that honesty with God about what we are feeling and how we are failing is worth any number of prize goats or a £20 note on the offerings plate.

Reflection

'God loves a cheerful giver' (2 Corinthians 9:7). Am I one of those or a grudging giver?

Veronica Zundel

Waiting for God

> See, I am sending my messenger to prepare the way before me, and the Lord whom you seek will suddenly come to his temple. The messenger of the covenant in whom you delight—indeed, he is coming, says the Lord of hosts. But who can endure the day of his coming, and who can stand when he appears? For he is like a refiner's fire and like fullers' soap; he will sit as a refiner and puri-fier of silver, and he will purify the descendants of Levi and refine them like gold and silver, until they present offerings to the Lord in righteousness. Then the offering of Judah and Jerusalem will be pleasing to the Lord as in the days of old and as in former years.

A church friend of mine recently went to a 'Sunday Assembly', the grow-ing movement in which atheists gather on a Sunday to hear talks and sing songs. He said that it was 'just like a Christian service, only without God'. Some Christian events can feel like that, too—we do all the right things, but it is as if God does not show up. Maybe God is too busy working in the world to turn up at our carefully organised services!

Of course, God is everywhere at all times, but we may fill our lives with so much clutter that we do not have space to feel the presence of God. What might happen if we stopped for a moment and just waited for God?

Well, it might not be all sweetness and light. Malachi's prophecy portrays God's coming as a scary event, after which things can never be the same again. Writer Annie Dillard suggests we need to wear crash helmets in church, if we really expect God to arrive. The idea of God as 'a refiner's fire' (v. 2) should make us prepared for pain as well as joy, as God burns out our selfishness and faults. Is it not worth it, though, if the end result is that we are like purest precious metal, serving God without any reservations?

Reflection

"Safe?" said Mr Beaver. "… [Aslan] isn't safe. But he's good. He's the King, I tell you."

C.S. Lewis, *The Lion, the Witch and the Wardrobe*

VERONICA ZUNDEL

Paul and the church

Concern and care for the church as a universal body, and for the individual churches that he had founded and continued to nurture, run through Paul's letters. There is no one place where he sets out a systematic theology of the church. Rather, his theology arises from the particular situations with which he is dealing. So, all the time, we need to be asking about a given teaching, 'Is this fundamental or is it specific to this group in this place?' Even the specific teaching might, however, with some translation, have things to teach us now in our own church settings and situations.

With so much material available, the passages and thoughts that follow can only be a snapshot. They do not, for example, cover the organisation of the church and its ministries, except in passing. They do, however, cover two key dimensions: how the church is to be in relation to God and in relation to the world.

With the first, we have what may be familiar metaphors of the church as body, bride, family, temple and the idea of being 'in Christ' that underlies many of them. With the second we have the vocation to be an intentional community, called out of the world, to witness to unity and equality, and be a place of reconciliation. Alongside both, we have Paul's great love for the church and, at times, his equal frustration and even anger when individuals and groups seem slow to grasp his teaching and put it into practice.

It can all seem a long way from our own experience of the church, but Richard P. McBrien, writing in *A New Dictionary of Christian Theology* (Alan Richardson and John Bowden, eds, 2009), identifies five common elements in all the New Testament churches, including Paul's, and these might be good means of assessing our own churches against his writings. Despite all their differences and difficulties, they shared 'faith in Jesus as Messiah and Lord; the practice of baptism and the celebration of the eucharist; the apostolic preaching and instruction; the high regard for communal love; and the expectation of the coming kingdom of God.' How does your church measure up?

Helen Julian CSF

1 CORINTHIANS 1:1–3 (NRSV)

Whose church is it anyway?

Paul, called to be an apostle of Christ Jesus by the will of God, and our brother Sosthenes, To the church of God that is in Corinth, to those who are sanctified in Christ Jesus, called to be saints, together with all those who in every place call on the name of our Lord Jesus Christ, both their Lord and ours: Grace to you and peace from God our Father and the Lord Jesus Christ.

This is the sort of passage, at the beginning of an epistle, that we will mostly pass over swiftly, on our way to its 'real' substance. In fact, the beginning tells us a lot about how Paul thinks of the church.

Notice that he does not refer to 'the Corinthian church' but to 'the church of God that is in Corinth' (v. 2). The church does not belong to its members, nor to the place in which they live. It is 'the church of God' and this is a theme that runs throughout the following passages, too. The word translated as 'church' is, in Greek, *ekklesia*, which means simply 'assembly'. So, it is of the essence of the church there that it gathers together; there is no church unless God's people assemble.

This gathering is both local and much wider than that—*ekklesia* is used to refer to a single local assembly, the churches of a region and to the whole church of God, expressed in these local and regional groups. Whichever is being used, the reference is always to a group of people, not a building, as there were no dedicated church buildings until long after Paul was writing.

What unites all these groups is their common calling. As Paul had been called to be an apostle by Christ Jesus, so the members of the church in Corinth had been called to be saints. They were and we are also part of the greater church, 'all those who in every place call on the name of our Lord Jesus Christ'.

Reflection

If you are going to church today, reflect where your sense of belonging comes from. As a Christian, do you belong to the building, the people who worship in it or primarily to the church throughout the world?

HELEN JULIAN CSF

Building a church

> After this Paul left Athens and went to Corinth. There he found a
> Jew named Aquila, a native of Pontus, who had recently come from
> Italy with his wife Priscilla, because Claudius had ordered all Jews
> to leave Rome. Paul went to see them, and, because he was of the
> same trade, he stayed with them, and they worked together—by
> trade they were tentmakers. Every sabbath he would argue in the
> synagogue and would try to convince Jews and Greeks.

If you went to church as a child, you may well have wiled away a dull
sermon idly inspecting a map of Paul's missionary journeys. The different lines show him crisscrossing the Mediterranean and ending up in
Rome. Today's passage fills out that broader picture and shows how
Paul went about founding local churches, some of which we know
about from his letters. Here we see the beginning of the Corinthian
church. Corinth was a port city, 60 kilometres from Athens, and a
Roman colony with many religious cults and a reputation for debauch-
ery. It was not an easy place in which to proclaim the good news.

The majority of Paul's early coworkers were Jewish converts to
Christianity and it is likely that Aquila and Priscilla fell into this camp.
They became important missionaries in their own right, travelling with
Paul to Syria and on to Ephesus (18:18–19). Their greetings are sent to
the church in Corinth (1 Corinthians 16:19) and they are greeted by
Paul (Romans 16:3; 2 Timothy 4:19). Although Paul seems the dominant figure, in fact he worked with many others in founding and nurturing churches, including those who travelled with him and those he left
behind to care for the fledgling communities.

Another regular practice that we can see here is his attendance at the
synagogue, where he seeks to persuade Jewish believers to accept
Christ. Week by week he would have built relationships, both there and
via his tentmaking. He often committed himself to a place for months
or even years. In today's terminology, this was incarnational mission.

Reflection

*Do you know who founded your church? Can you remember the first
person who spoke to you about Jesus? Give thanks for them today.*

HELEN JULIAN CSF

Wide open heart

We have spoken frankly to you Corinthians; our heart is wide open to you. There is no restriction in our affections, but only in yours. In return—I speak as to children—open wide your hearts also... Make room in your hearts for us; we have wronged no one, we have corrupted no one, we have taken advantage of no one. I do not say this to condemn you, for I said before that you are in our hearts, to die together and to live together. I often boast about you; I have great pride in you; I am filled with consolation; I am overjoyed in all our affliction.

Not surprisingly, given his commitment to their 'birth', Paul had strong feelings about 'his' churches. Even when everything was not going well, he expressed great affection towards them and worked hard to restore good relations.

The background here is that, after Paul wrote his first letter, addressing some problems in their church life, he heard that there were further problems and visited again on his way to Macedonia. It was a painful visit, with open opposition to him, led by one member in particular. After he had left, Paul sent Titus with a very strong letter (2 Corinthians 2:3–4). It caused him anguish to write it, but he assures the church that he wrote it, 'not to cause you pain, but to let you know the abundant love that I have for you' (2:4b). The letter had the desired effect (7:6–7) and Paul wrote his second letter to the Corinthians in response to this news. You can read Paul's retelling of this process in 1:1—2:13.

Today's brief passages echo each other in their appeal for an open-hearted response to Paul's love for the Christians in Corinth. Here, he assures them that he knows they think no evil of him (7:3) and he speaks well of them to others. Even the difficulties they have experienced, their 'affliction', makes him 'overjoyed' (v. 4)—a very emphatic word. The freedom they share in Christ enables them to share thoughts and emotions openly.

Reflection

How well does your church handle difficult situations? Pray today to love the church, with all its imperfections.

Helen Julian CSF

A contrary gospel

Paul an apostle—sent neither by human commission nor from human authorities, but through Jesus Christ and God the Father, who raised him from the dead—and all the members of God's family who are with me... I am astonished that you are so quickly deserting the one who called you in the grace of Christ and are turning to a different gospel—not that there is another gospel, but there are some who are confusing you and want to pervert the gospel of Christ. But even if we or an angel from heaven should proclaim to you a gospel contrary to what we proclaimed to you, let that one be accursed!

Not every dispute was settled with as much good grace as that with the Corinthians. Here, Paul has barely begun his letter before he is berating the Galatians. Where there would normally be thanksgiving, there is powerful criticism.

The background seems to be that, in Paul's absence, another group of Christians had come to Galatia, preaching that the gospel message made it possible for Gentiles to become full members of the people of Israel—but only if they kept the Law and the men were circumcised. Paul saw this as unacceptable, a backward move away from faith and towards justification by works of the Law. While he certainly wanted both Jews and Gentiles to be equally at home in the church and in other places urged mutual toleration, this was a step too far. It was moving away from what was, for Paul, central to the very existence of the churches—their foundation on Christ and faith in him as Messiah and Lord. He would battle against anything that detracted from this.

I find it comforting in a strange way that the church has always strayed. Even this very early group of Christians, so close to Jesus' time and founded and taught by Paul himself, were tempted by teaching that, perhaps, seemed easier to keep than the life of faith taught by Paul. Also, that Paul was human enough to be hurt and angry by it.

Reflection

What is central to your gospel? What would cause you to make a stand as Paul did?

HELEN JULIAN CSF

One body, many gifts

For just as the body is one and has many members, and all the members of the body, though many, are one body, so it is with Christ. For in the one Spirit we were all baptised into one body—Jews or Greeks, slaves or free—and we were made to drink of one Spirit. Indeed, the body does not consist of one member but of many... Now you are the body of Christ and individually members of it.

This is one of the most well-known ways in which Paul described the church—as the body of Christ. This latter part of 1 Corinthians is the first place in which it is used, so here we are at the birthplace of an important metaphor and the most extended treatment of it. Paul also refers to it briefly in Romans 12:4–5, Ephesians 4:12 and Colossians 1:18.

Paul draws on the political world around him for this image, though he uses it in a distinctive and quite complex way. The beginning of 1 Corinthians 12 is on the gifts of the Spirit. Different gifts are given to each, but all are 'for the common good' (v. 7) and given by the same God. This unity in diversity is then spelled out in the image of the body. All the baptised, wherever they have come from, have received the same Spirit and this has made them members of the one body. Hence, they are united both to one another and to Christ.

Therefore, the church's identity cannot be separated from that of Christ. Once again, we see the centrality of Christ to Paul's teaching to his churches—everything else revolves around him and what he has done. The amazing claim in this passage, however, is that, when Christians come together, Christ is truly present. Notice the emphasis on all the parts coming 'together'. As we saw earlier, the church (the *ekklesia*/assembly) exists in coming together and it is 'you' (plural) who are the body of Christ to his world.

Reflection

Prayerfully, read the whole of chapter 12 and ask for God's guidance to discern which is your gift in the body of the church. It may be a gift you already exercise or perhaps you are called to something new.

HELEN JULIAN CSF

Creator and ruler

Christ is the image of the invisible God, the firstborn of all creation; for in him all things in heaven and on earth were created, things visible and invisible, whether thrones or dominions or rulers or powers— all things have been created through him and for him. He himself is before all things, and in him all things hold together. He is the head of the body, the church; he is the beginning, the firstborn from the dead, so that he might come to have first place in everything.

Here we have the Colossian version of yesterday's Corinthian passage, which also described the church as being like a body, and it offers a new take on this image. We often pray in church for our leaders—bishops, archbishops, the Pope or more local leaders in our church—but here we are presented with a powerful image of the real leader and head of the church—Christ, 'the firstborn of all creation' (v. 15).

Verses 15–20 have a rhythmic structure and may perhaps have been a hymn. They also echo the content of the creed as they speak of the role of Christ in creation (vv. 15–17) and redemption (vv. 18–20). From the local disputes and difficulties of some of our earlier readings, we have moved on to explore a much more cosmic place, in which Christ is the pivotal point, the 'firstborn' of both creation and the new order of redemption, 'firstborn from the dead' (v. 18).

The Greek title *arche*, which is translated as 'head' here, could be used of political leaders, but is never used of leaders in the church— only of Christ or other lesser supernatural beings (for example, in 1 Corinthians 2:6, 8, where it is part of the phrase 'rulers of this age').

The 'all things' that Paul repeatedly affirms to be subservient to Christ included all kinds of powers, celestial and earthly, including the angelic beings who were important in contemporary Jewish writings. With Christ as head, his body, the church, need not fear anything, visible or invisible.

Prayer

Christ our Lord, image of the invisible God, firstborn of all creation, lead your body, the church, to know you as their head and give you first place in everything.

HELEN JULIAN CSF

Bride and bridegroom

Husbands, love your wives, just as Christ loved the church and gave himself up for her, in order to make her holy by cleansing her with the washing of water by the word, so as to present the church to himself in splendour, without a spot or wrinkle or anything of the kind—yes, so that she may be holy and without blemish. In the same way, husbands should love their wives as they do their own bodies... This is a great mystery, and I am applying it to Christ and the church.

This entire passage from Ephesians (5:21–33) on the relationship between a husband and wife has its difficulties and many struggle with it today. Within it, however, we find this image of the church as the bride of Christ, which is worth considering on its own. From the cosmic imagery of Colossians, with Christ as the head, above all things, we move to a much more intimate picture of Christ, as the bridegroom to a beloved bride.

I recently read a novel about the wedding of an ultra-Orthodox Jewish couple. Before the marriage, the bride to be took a careful ritual bath, the *mikveh*. This involved submerging herself entirely several times while reciting set prayers. For Jewish Christians, there may well have been echoes of this ritual in their baptism, which would normally then have been by total immersion. Both involve water with the word.

The husband in this passage is head of the wife as Christ is head of the church, so where we see 'husband' we can also see 'Christ'. The germ of this idea is perhaps in 2 Corinthians 11:2, where Paul writes, 'I promised you in marriage to one husband.' The analogy breaks down somewhat in the middle, where it seems that Christ as bridegroom presents the bride to himself—a very strange wedding!

The idea of the church as a bride to Christ, her bridegroom, however, does help us to think of the unity between Christ and his church, the devotion that the church owes Christ and the loving care that Christ has for the church.

Reflection

Do you find this a useful image? Reflect on the reasons for your answer.

HELEN JULIAN CSF

Family of God

We know that all things work together for good for those who love God, who are called according to his purpose. For those whom he foreknew he also predestined to be conformed to the image of his Son, in order that he might be the firstborn within a large family. And those whom he predestined he also called; and those whom he called he also justified; and those whom he justified he also glorified.

Not all of us are married, but the majority are or have been part of families of some kind. Once again, as so often with Paul's imagery, Christ is central. We are called to become more and more like Christ, 'conformed to the image of his [God's] Son' (v. 29) and, hence, to become members of his family. It is another facet of being 'heirs, heirs of God and joint heirs with Christ' (8:17). This process is so certain that Paul writes of this future glorification in the past tense. From God's standpoint and in God's purpose it has, in a sense, already happened, so what we have to do is live more and more into the reality of it.

The church is not, of course, a biological family. Its members become children of God via their baptism, when they receive 'a spirit of adoption' (8:15). There is continuity with Judaism—Abraham is 'our father' (4:1)—but also discontinuity, as we have a new relationship with God as father through Jesus Christ. Further, although this is not a biological family, the bonds formed by the Holy Spirit are real and strong. Believers are 'brothers and sisters', an idea that strengthens the community's identity and unity. In Paul's time, the relationship between brothers was the supreme paradigm for fellowship, so this language of kinship encouraged the growth of fellowship in the new church body.

Of course, not all our experiences of family are happy ones, so we may bring into the church, experienced as family, both positive and negative expectations. We need, then, to ask the Holy Spirit to strengthen the good and heal the bad.

Reflection

How has your experience of family shaped your relationships with fellow Christians in the church, for good and for bad?

HELEN JULIAN CSF

Chosen and called

Blessed be the God and Father of our Lord Jesus Christ, who has blessed us in Christ with every spiritual blessing in the heavenly places, just as he chose us in Christ before the foundation of the world to be holy and blameless before him in love. He destined us for adoption as his children through Jesus Christ, according to the good pleasure of his will, to the praise of his glorious grace that he freely bestowed on us in the Beloved.

'Friends are God's apology for relations' runs author Hugh Kingsmill's famous saying. Most of us as children probably wished we belonged to some other family—where the house was bigger, the parents kinder and the food better.

There is a high value placed on choice today—choice of school, hospital and, in many ways, identity. Choice is also crucial here, but it is God's choice, not ours: 'He chose us in Christ' (v. 4). This may seem to obliterate the possibility of making our own choice, but, for Paul, this is cause for rejoicing. Verses 3–14 are one long paragraph about all the wonderful things that God has done for us in Christ and his blessings for us are closely linked with his choosing us.

There are, of course, difficulties in this concept—why would some be chosen and not others? In church history, there is much evidence of theological cul de sacs based on this and other similar passages. It is possible, however, to see this as an expression of God's overall desire for his people—in Christ all are chosen and called. The church is to be the body of those who have heard and accepted this call, receiving baptism, becoming children of God and brothers and sisters of Christ and, hence, the privileges of belonging to God's family.

So, this is not a cause for pride, but thanksgiving and humility. It is also a new way of thinking of the church. It is not like a club that we join (and may leave), something we can shape to our desires. Rather, it is something that shapes us into God's holy people.

Reflection

How does the idea of being chosen affect your view of the church and your belonging to it?

HELEN JULIAN CSF

A promise kept

I am speaking the truth in Christ—I am not lying... I have great sorrow and unceasing anguish in my heart. For I could wish that I myself were accursed and cut off from Christ for the sake of my own people, my kindred according to the flesh... It is not as though the word of God had failed. For not all Israelites truly belong to Israel, and not all of Abraham's children are his true descendants; but 'It is through Isaac that descendants shall be named after you.' This means that it is not the children of the flesh who are the children of God, but the children of the promise are counted as descendants.

If the church is the body of those chosen and called, what has become of the people already chosen and called, the people of the covenant, the Israelites? Romans 9—11 shows us Paul (himself, of course, one of those chosen people) wrestling with this agonising question. Has God abandoned his people?

Paul's basic belief is announced in verse 6a: 'It is not as though the word of God had failed.' Towards the end of the chapters, too, there is a similar declaration: 'for the gifts and the calling of God are irrevocable' (11:29). Paul works out his argument within these two core beliefs.

In order to do this, he has to acknowledge that there has been failure. Many of God's people have not kept the covenant or have misunderstood it. As in the early days, when Abraham had two sons, Ishmael and Isaac, it was only through Isaac's line that the promise descended to the future. This is part of a longer history of election and rejection (9:6–29), in which Paul invokes the idea of the faithful 'remnant' (11:1–6) to identify himself with other believing Jews who have remained faithful and are therefore 'children of the promise' (9:8).

Seeing the church as the fulfilment of God's promise, not replacing Israel but bringing it to completion, is an important part of Paul's vision.

Prayer

Faithful God, thank you that your calling is for all time. Make us grateful for our long history with you.

HELEN JULIAN CSF

Where God dwells

So [Jesus] came and proclaimed peace to you who were far off and peace to those who were near; for through him both of us have access in one Spirit to the Father. So then you are no longer strangers and aliens, but you are citizens with the saints and also members of the household of God, built upon the foundation of the apostles and prophets, with Christ Jesus himself as the cornerstone. In him the whole structure is joined together and grows into a holy temple in the Lord; in whom you also are built together spiritually into a dwelling place for God.

This passage draws on the distinction between Jew and Gentile with which we wrestled yesterday, but with a happier and more positive outcome. It introduces another of Paul's images for the church—the building or temple and a variation of the family, 'the household' (v. 19).

There is no longer a division between Gentiles ('who were far off', v. 17) and God; and Jews who accept Jesus have the same access to the Father. The same Spirit dwells in all of them and us, and all can have the same peace with God. This was a major change. When only the people of Israel were God's people, the Gentiles, even those living in Jewish territory, were resident aliens, with no rights as citizens, but now they have full and equal rights. Further, these very diverse people are all being built into a single 'building', housing a single 'household'.

In those times, the household was an extended group, including relatives, servants and slaves. Again, here we see diversity and unity. Also, the early church did not have buildings set aside for worship, but met within the households of its wealthier members, so this would have been a familiar experience to Paul's audience.

It is not just a household, however, but also a temple. It is not a physical building, but the place of God's presence, where God builds his people into a place where he dwells, as they meet to worship and to have fellowship with one another.

Reflection

What is needed to build your church more fully into such a temple for God's presence?

HELEN JULIAN CSF

1 THESSALONIANS 5:11, 14–19 (NRSV)

Working at community

Therefore encourage one another and build up each other, as indeed you are doing... And we urge you, beloved, to admonish the idlers, encourage the faint-hearted, help the weak, be patient with all of them. See that none of you repays evil for evil, but always seek to do good to one another and to all. Rejoice always, pray without ceasing, give thanks in all circumstances; for this is the will of God in Christ Jesus for you. Do not quench the Spirit.

As a member of a religious community, I know that people can have romantic and unrealistic ideas about what community life is like. Sometimes they imagine that we all agree, all get on well with each other at all times, never fall out. A moment's thought about family life or, indeed, church life would show that this is unlikely.

Even the church, the body of Christ, the temple where God dwells, has to work at the quality of its life together. As a body, bound together by the commitment of its members to Christ and, hence, to one another, it cannot rely on the ties of kinship to get it through hard times and disagreement. So encouragement and a mutual building up are central. Here, Paul spells out some of what that might look like.

Paul, however, also knows that sometimes it is necessary to take issue with people's behaviour. Here he mentions 'idlers', which might better be translated as 'disorderly'—those who stand against order on principle. Not a helpful attitude for life together.

He commends far more encouragement and forbearance be shown to those who are struggling or even going against community norms. That is because, as the Christians in Thessalonica build each other up, they will also be building up the body and the temple. Hence, they will be allowing the work of the Spirit to flourish in the church and overflow into the society around them.

Prayer

God of the church, you call us to live together in love and encouragement,
forbearance and accountability. Give us a deep commitment to one another
and a willingness to work through difficulties with patience and love, so the
world may see our joy and believe in you.

HELEN JULIAN CSF

All one in Christ

Therefore the law was our disciplinarian until Christ came, so that we might be justified by faith. But now that faith has come, we are no longer subject to a disciplinarian, for in Christ Jesus you are all children of God through faith. As many of you as were baptised into Christ have clothed yourself with Christ. There is no longer Jew or Greek, there is no longer slave or free, there is no longer male and female; for all of you are one in Christ Jesus. And if you belong to Christ, then you are Abraham's offspring, heirs according to the promise.

Here Paul restates some themes that we have already seen—we are children of God and inheritors of the promise made to Abraham. In the middle, he makes an astonishing claim—that, in Christ, the three key distinctions of his times have been abolished. There are differing views among commentators on whether it is unity that is the priority here or equality. It is a radical claim in either case, and remains so. Ethnic, economic and gender divisions are still powerful in today's world.

The context is important, too. Paul was writing to a community of Gentiles where some were seeking circumcision—a mark of 'belonging' that gave Jews and males a higher status than Gentiles and women. They needed to hear that, in baptism, these marks of status had been washed away and they belonged to one another in all their variety.

Of course, in other places, Paul seems to contradict himself—he is always writing to particular situations. He still identifies himself as a Jew (2:15; Romans 9:1–5; Philippians 3:3–6); slavery still exists (1 Corinthians 7:21–22); and gender still matters (1 Corinthians 11:2–16).

The Law, which had been the guarantee of the promise, had acted as a disciplinarian—the slave who escorted young men to school and back so they would not get into trouble. Now that Christ has come, it is no longer necessary; the young men have 'grown up' and, in baptism, the promise is available to all, in faith.

Reflection

How, and to what extent, does your church community model radical unity and equality?

HELEN JULIAN CSF

Reconciled and reconciling

From now on, therefore, we regard no one from a human point of view; even though we once knew Christ from a human point of view, we know him no longer in that way. So if anyone is in Christ, there is a new creation: everything old has passed away; see, everything has become new! All this is from God, who reconciled us to himself through Christ, and has given us the ministry of reconciliation; that is, in Christ God was reconciling the world to himself, not counting their trespasses against them, and entrusting the message of reconciliation to us.

A community in which the divisions of society—ethnicity, status, gender—are no longer relevant was and still is something very new. God has taken the initiative in this, reconciling the world to himself through Christ. It is the task of the church now to share in this role, because the members of the church, and the church as a whole, are 'in Christ'.

The argument begins in verses 14 and 15, with a reorientation of the believer—because, in faith, they shared in the death of Christ and, therefore the life they now lived was to be lived for and in Christ. This was a fundamentally different way of looking at the world (v. 16), and leads to the glorious promise of verse 17: 'if anyone is in Christ, there is a new creation'. This does not mean that the original person has been wiped out, but, instead, renewed and so lives by different standards.

Of course, this was not to happen all at once. Later in this letter, it is obvious that Paul's converts are still impressed by power and eloquence (ch. 11). The new life and its values have to be lived into. Even while this is happening, however, they are to be agents and ambassadors of reconciliation and this image of the ambassador continues until 6:2. As God's ambassadors, we are to offer his gift of peace to the world and model it ourselves, however imperfectly.

Prayer

God of love, you reconcile us to yourself and make us new creations in your Son. Send us out to offer this gift to your world.

HELEN JULIAN CSF

Christmas: good news for the poor

The more I read the scriptures, the more I come to appreciate the significant relationship between the birth narratives in the New Testament and God's promises to 'the ancestors' that run through the Old Testament. In the birth narratives, the Saviour and Messiah is born, the good news of liberation is proclaimed and the people rejoice. They also begin a new journey, one that will involve struggle and pain as well as celebration.

In so many ways, the stories surrounding the birth of Jesus set the scene for the whole of the gospel story, proclaiming that Israel is finally redeemed and deliverance opened to all peoples. History, however, has shown us how humanity continues to 'mess it all up'. The promised redemption and deliverance—at least on earth—is too often blocked by injustice, cruelty and conflict. The memory of Christmas enshrined in the stories surrounding Jesus' birth, however, keeps alive the hopes for and the commitment to the as yet unfulfilled possibilities that the birth inaugurated, the kingdom of God that is yet to be fully revealed.

My reading of these stories tells me the promise of redemption and deliverance is not something that awaits us only at 'the end of time', but, rather, is an experience for the present moment—for the here and now! So many of the biblical stories were told or written not simply to provide information about the past but also to offer patterns of hope and trust in the fulfilment of God's promises—to offer liberation.

It is in this context that I will travel through the well-known stories that tell of the birth of Jesus. Fundamentally, they are stories about liberation. In and through that birth, God inaugurated the long-awaited deliverance of his people.

One of my concerns about this time of year is the way in which too many people domesticate the Christmas story into a festival of gift-giving consumption, legitimated by the symbol of Santa Claus. Once freed from that domesticating atmosphere, whereby Christmas is no more than 'the winter holiday', the stories of the first Christmas can be read for what they truly are—astonishing stories of God's liberating initiative to set his children free once and for all.

Andrew Jones

A gift for all people

In the beginning was the Word, and the Word was with God, and the Word was God... And the Word became flesh and lived among us, and we have seen his glory, the glory as of a father's only son, full of grace and truth.

Nudging the world away from domesticating the powerful good news of the gospel is an urgent task. This is true not only in relation to the birth narratives but also for so much of the New Testament—the Beatitudes, the healing miracles, the kingdom message in the parables, the cross and the resurrection.

At the heart of that task lies the truth concerning Christ's divinity, which is why I believe the church has traditionally linked the opening verses of John's Gospel with Christmas. These verses celebrate the power that lies behind the assertion that the one whose birth we celebrate on Christmas Day was none other than the pre-existent Word, whose activity was in creation (vv. 1–5) and in enlightening human beings (vv. 9–12), enabling us to share in the divine life (vv. 14–16).

For me, the greatest achievement of these verses is the way in which they establish the divinity of Jesus and place him firmly in a filial relationship with God. This takes us further—this filial relationship is compatible with the reality of God's reign over the whole world. From the perspective of liberation, therefore, this fully filial relationship between God and Christ, which is revealed to us anew each Christmas, is a powerful proclamation that, in the manger, we gaze at the definitive mediator of the reign of God.

To domesticate this truth is to be content only to sing about it. Believing fully in it means being concerned with the intolerable brokenness of our world, caused by countless injustices. Believing fully in the coming of God's reign through the manger also means being unavoidably committed to tackling the reality of dehumanising poverty and holding on to the hope of its eradication.

Reflection

In God's reign, the risen, ascended, glorified Christ is also the Jesus of the Bethlehem manger.

ANDREW JONES

Joseph and a potential disgrace

Now the birth of Jesus the Messiah took place in this way. When his mother Mary had been engaged to Joseph, but before they lived together, she was found to be with child from the Holy Spirit. Her husband Joseph, being a righteous man and unwilling to expose her to public disgrace, planned to dismiss her quietly. But just when he had resolved to do this, an angel of the Lord appeared to him in a dream and said, 'Joseph, son of David, do not be afraid to take Mary as your wife, for the child conceived in her is from the Holy Spirit. She will bear a son, and you are to name him Jesus.'

The area in which I work includes five schools and, along with some other people, I have quite a busy and rewarding ministry there. Naturally, Christmas is an exciting time for children, especially as the Christmas term comes to a close, with parties, concerts, carols, crib services and, of course, the Christmas tree!

During recent years, I have adopted the practice of collecting old Christmas cards and storing them in themed shoe boxes, with a box for Mary, one for the shepherds, one for the Magi and one for the angels. Each year in early December, I choose a box as my theme for the schools. I get the children to examine the cards and reflect, in very simple terms, on the different faces, clothes, backgrounds and so forth, trying to draw out what they make of the characters who play such crucial parts in the nativity scene.

My aim is to show that these are not 'cardboard cut-outs', but real people, who have a continuing ministry through the retelling of that powerful story. These are people who convey eternal values and, as such, should not be seen as somehow figures of myth.

Today, it is Joseph's turn to be centre stage and, in these verses, we remember the way in which, through God's power, he was able to turn a potential ruin into love; to transform disgrace into grace, thus enabling life to flourish.

Reflection

Daily we too have opportunities to be Josephs, pulling those in need from the ruins of life and offering them grace.

ANDREW JONES

The young girl rejoices

And Mary said, 'My soul magnifies the Lord, and my spirit rejoices in God my Saviour, for he has looked with favour on the lowliness of his servant. Surely, from now on all generations will call me blessed; for the Mighty One has done great things for me, and holy is his name. His mercy is for those who fear him from generation to generation.'

Last year, I had the privilege of writing a book on Mary (*Mary: A gospel witness to transfiguration and liberation*, BRF, 2014), which was the fruit of two years or so of investigating the context of Mary's life and ministry. It was an amazing journey of discovery, which started when I was invited to lead a pilgrimage to Montserrat, Spain's most famous Marian shrine. During the few days I spent there, I asked the pilgrims to compare the way in which the church has built an enormous edifice of tradition around the figure of Mary—shrines, basilicas, doctrines, hymns and so on—with what is a strikingly thin collection of evidence in the New Testament. For most of the pilgrims this came as a surprise and many of them kept saying that there must be much more to it than that! It was the search for that 'much more' which led me to research Mary.

Probably her song, which we call the 'Magnificat', continues to be the most well known of all the references to Mary in the Gospels. It falls into two parts and, in many ways, the second part—highlighting a theme of liberation—eclipses the song's opening. The song begins with a sense of gratitude and acceptance of being such a key player in God's incarnation, the event that ushers in God's new, liberating reign. Like Mary, though, we must agree to be part of God's great project of liberation. Mary's 'Yes' was an expression of faith and the abiding challenge of her 'Yes' for us is that our own 'Yes' to God, here and now, must also be deeply rooted in faith.

Reflection

We can begin to make our 'Yes' a reality by emptying ourselves of prejudice and hypocrisy. Only in this way can our service to others be genuine and not condescending.

ANDREW JONES

Power versus mercy

'He has shown strength with his arm; he has scattered the proud in the thoughts of their hearts. He has brought down the powerful from their thrones, and lifted up the lowly; he has filled the hungry with good things, and sent the rich away empty. He has helped his servant Israel, in remembrance of his mercy, according to the promise he made to our ancestors, to Abraham and to his descendants for ever.'

In the stories and songs about the birth of Jesus, we hear of God acting for his people, in contrast to the tyrannical power of Caesar and Herod. The overwhelming emphasis, particularly in the first two chapters of Luke's Gospel, is that the birth of Jesus means salvation for the people and freedom from their enemies, but the implication of this is that raising up the lowly and feeding the hungry also means ejecting the mighty from their thrones and sending the rich away empty.

If we look back through other songs and stories in the Bible, we see further examples of God saying 'No!' to unjust rulers. In Exodus 15, God says 'No!' to Pharaoh, in Judges 5 he says 'No!' to the Canaanite kings. In 1 Kings 19 and 2 Kings 9, God says 'No!' to Ahab and Jezebel, while in Daniel 11, he says 'No!' to Antiochus Epiphanes.

Turning back to Luke 1 and 2, we can reflect that God continues to say 'No!' to today's Caesars. He continues to act on behalf of those who cry out in need and work tirelessly for peace and goodwill.

We should not forget either that, in the birth of Jesus, God also included an enormously important promise: peace on earth. It was that promise, I think, which would have particularly excited very ordinary people, such as Mary, Elizabeth, Simeon and Anna and the shepherds. Most of us, like them, are very ordinary people, too, called and challenged to be excited by that same promise and, like them, longing to see it fulfilled.

Reflection

In our Christmas preparations this year, we can pray to rediscover excitement, not for tinsel and trimmings, but the love which surely did come down that first Christmas—and for the promise of peace.

ANDREW JONES

The shepherds hear it first

In that region there were shepherds living in the fields, keeping watch over their flock by night. Then an angel of the Lord stood before them, and the glory of the Lord shone around them, and they were terrified. But the angel said to them, 'Do not be afraid; for see—I am bringing you good news of great joy for all people: to you is born this day in the city of David a Saviour, who is the Messiah, the Lord.'

Reading these verses always reminds me of the significance of David's humble origins as a shepherd (1 Samuel 16:1–3). God seems to have had a real soft spot for shepherds and the image of a shepherd as being significant runs through the whole of the Bible—Moses, David and Amos were not only shepherds but also some of them are recorded as being about their shepherding work when they encountered God.

In the New Testament, Jesus shared that same soft spot for shepherds—his parables are rich with this pastoral motif and Jesus even refers to himself as the good shepherd (John 10:11) and the gate for the sheep (10:7), while elsewhere he is, of course, described as the 'Lamb of God'. What is remarkable about this 'divine soft spot' is that, at the time, shepherds were considered lowly folk, to say the least. They were generally poor, unwashed and unclean—both physically and ritually—and lacked any hope of acceptability in religious terms.

During the course of today, Christmas Eve, we will hear again the story of the shepherds and sing their praises as being the very first to hear of the birth of Jesus—a birth that occurred among the same poverty and dirt as that in which the shepherds worked. This is all topsy-turvy stuff, but intimately connected with Luke's theme of joy in the face of God's salvation and his breaking into human history.

The shepherds, of course, responded eagerly to the message of the angel and approached the manger with awe (Luke:15–20).

Reflection

The shepherds walked with their sheep and we, too, are called to be shepherds of one another—guiding and giving to each other what we need to walk on confidently.

ANDREW JONES

The child is named

All this took place to fulfil what had been spoken by the Lord through the prophet: 'Look, the virgin shall conceive and bear a son, and they shall name him Emmanuel', which means, 'God is with us.' When Joseph awoke from sleep, he did as the angel of the Lord commanded him; he took her as his wife, but had no marital relations with her until she had borne a son; and he named him Jesus.

A very blessed Christmas to you all! When I ponder the glory of Christmas, I cannot help but think that the crib was a place of both encounter and meeting. It was there that divinity and humanity were reconciled and God and his people brought together in an unprecedented way, which opened up the possibility of this meeting becoming an eternal one.

Almost every year I get at least one card bearing the words 'Love came down at Christmas', which is exactly what the manger represented that day in Bethlehem. What happened changed the world and can still change the lives of all people everywhere. It is as if God, in his coming as Christ, poured divinity and holiness upon the world, but, at the same time, elevated humanity and reconciled it to himself. Christ is born so that God can become man and we can become holy.

Year after year, Christmas after Christmas, God finds new places of meeting for the divine and the human, to draw us together with him in love. To domesticate this means paying lip service to its power and potential to transform the world. It means singing the carols without allowing their words to turn each one of us upside down so that, instead of facing the tinsel and the trimmings, we face the newborn child himself and become immersed in his mission to transform the brokenness of our world.

Reflection

Jesus is God the Word living among us, not because we know a lot of interesting facts about him that prove he was the best man who ever lived, but because his life, death and resurrection make a drastic, once-and-for-all difference to the world and our lives.

ANDREW JONES

A 'powerful' man frightened by a child

In the time of King Herod, after Jesus was born in Bethlehem of Judea, wise men from the East came to Jerusalem, asking, 'Where is the child who has been born king of the Jews? For we observed his star at its rising, and have come to pay him homage.' When King Herod heard this, he was frightened, and all Jerusalem with him.

During the lifetime of Jesus, there were a number of rulers who bore the name Herod, including Herod Archelaus, Herod Antipas and Herod Philip. Perhaps the most famous of them was their father, Herod the Great, the 'wicked king' of the Christmas story (Matthew 2; Luke 1:5), who was King of the Jews (a title given to him by Rome) in the period between 37 and 4BC and completed the building of the second and last temple in Jerusalem.

He was a clever politician who, although he had the support of Rome and ruled efficiently, was also unpredictable and unscrupulous. At the very top of his agenda were his own personal interests and he was merciless when those interests were threatened. He killed one wife and two sons, as well as being the instigator of the massacre of the Holy Innocents, which we remember on 28 December.

As Jesus was born during the reign of this Herod, it was at his palace that the Magi enquired as to the whereabouts of the birth of the 'true' King of the Jews—hence, today's verses state that Herod was frightened.

The first-century Jewish historian Flavius Josephus described Herod as being deluded, violent and vicious. Despite his political acumen, consummate diplomacy and cruelty, he was frightened when confronted by truth. Is this not how it has always been and continues to be today? The truth does set people free (John 8:32), but will also inevitably threaten all that is unjust.

Reflection

Today the church remembers Stephen, the first Christian martyr, who was stoned to death for standing up faithfully for the truth. As we continue to celebrate Christmas, let us also pause to remember those who are still persecuted today for their faith in Christ.

ANDREW JONES

Strange gifts for a newborn babe

When [the wise men] saw that the star had stopped, they were overwhelmed with joy. On entering the house, they saw the child with Mary his mother; and they knelt down and paid him homage. Then, opening their treasure-chests, they offered him gifts of gold, frankincense, and myrrh.

The Magi (or 'wise men') continued their journey from Herod's palace and eventually arrived in Bethlehem. They recognised the one for whom they had been searching and worshipped him. It is the nature of their gifts, however, that fascinates me—the gold, frankincense and myrrh.

Gold has two sides to it—it is a symbol of wealth and power, but also of greed and selfishness. Then, as today, people killed for gold; because of gold, people constructed edifices of injustice, degradation and oppression. Frankincense symbolises the rising up of prayer and devotion, the lifting of our aspirations and hopes to heaven. Myrrh is the symbol of suffering and pain. Is this not why one of the Magi in T.S. Eliot's poem 'Journey of the Magi' returned home wondering what he had seen—was it a birth or a death? Clearly, from the very beginning of the gospel story, Christmas and Easter, incarnation and resurrection, manger and cross are meant to be seen as one.

Could we not perhaps say that there is a fourth Magi in the story— you and me? What gifts do we bring? Let the gold we offer be our hope that wealth can be distributed justly and used with justice today. Let the frankincense we offer be our hope that members of different traditions and cultures grow to recognise the way in which God has bestowed dignity and rights on all. Let the myrrh we offer be our prayer that people become more and more willing to share the sufferings of others and ease the pain and loneliness that too many struggle with today.

Reflection

*As we approach the end of the year and the start of a new one,
let us pray for gifts of generosity, gratitude and gentleness so that we
become a people who are generous with words and thoughts, grateful to
and for each other and gentle with those we love, with those we encounter
anew and with our world.*

ANDREW JONES

Massacre, devastation and injustice

Now after [the wise men] had left, an angel of the Lord appeared to Joseph in a dream and said, 'Get up, take the child and his mother, and flee to Egypt, and remain there until I tell you; for Herod is about to search for the child, to destroy him.' Then Joseph got up, took the child and his mother by night, and went to Egypt, and remained there until the death of Herod. This was to fulfil what had been spoken by the Lord through the prophet, 'Out of Egypt I have called my son.' When Herod saw that he had been tricked by the wise men, he was infuriated, and he sent and killed all the children in and around Bethlehem who were two years old or under.

Having been warned in a dream of Herod's intention to destroy Jesus, Joseph flees with his family to Egypt and they become refugees. The mention of Egypt has a deep spiritual significance, with the quotation used by Matthew (v. 15) coming from Hosea 11:1 as a reminder of the fundamental experience of salvation—the Exodus from Egyptian bondage. The 'son' in the prophecy is Israel, the people of God, and Matthew here applies the exodus experience to Jesus, suggesting that, in this birth, we begin to see the start of the new and full restoration of the people of God. The flight to Egypt can be seen as a new and different type of exodus, but this time with a new and greater Moses.

What rapidly followed this exodus was the massacre of all male children of two years old and under within the district and town of Bethlehem. Herod acts in character and the story is reminiscent of Pharaoh's command to kill the male offspring of the Israelites (Exodus 1:16), both of which are genocidal acts and a complete abuse of power.

Reflection
Tragically, genocide still happens in our world, as does the serious abuse of power. If only all rulers could recognise the true giver of human power and learn to use it as a gift to serve the common good. As we remember the massacre of the innocent children of Bethlehem, let us pray today for all children who face life-threatening situations, for whatever reason.

ANDREW JONES

Liberation for refugees

When Herod died, an angel of the Lord suddenly appeared in a dream to Joseph in Egypt and said, 'Get up, take the child and his mother, and go to the land of Israel, for those who were seeking the child's life are dead.'

Once Herod had died, Matthew records that the holy family returned to Nazareth. Once again, we have an important connection with the exodus. Verse 20 is reminiscent of Exodus 4:19, in which, following Moses' experience at the burning bush and God's call to him to help free his people from the bondage of Egypt, he decides to accept the challenge and return to Egypt. God tells him, 'Go back to Egypt; for all those who were seeking your life are dead.' Just as Moses was able to return from Midian to Egypt and begin the process of saving his people, so Jesus returns from Egypt (after Herod's death) to Israel where he, too, will save his people.

During the past few days, our Bible passages have confronted us with some seriously traumatic stuff. No sooner had the birthday celebrations, as it were, got going, than Joseph, Mary and Jesus had to pack their bags and run for their lives. Today they get the chance to return— and what a journey that must have been! I wonder how reliable Joseph thought that dream really was?

Packing bags and running for your life is a tragically familiar story in our own times. We are only too aware that Christmas for countless millions of refugees today continues to be an apparently endless round of hunger, thirst, separation, longing and fear. The journeys we have read about in the last few days, however, from Nazareth to Bethlehem, Bethlehem to Egypt and then back again to Nazareth, and all that happened as part of those journeys, should encourage us to keep looking for fresh signs of God at work, despite human turmoil and trouble.

Reflection

Where do we look for those fresh signs? Among the innocent victims of our crazy world, in the stillness of those who submit their lives in love to God and in the protests against injustice of those who practise Christian service without counting the cost.

ANDREW JONES

A home at last

But when [Joseph] heard that Archelaus was ruling over Judea in place of his father Herod, he was afraid to go there. And after being warned in a dream, he went away to the district of Galilee. There he made his home in a town called Nazareth, so that what had been spoken through the prophets might be fulfilled, 'He will be called a Nazorean.'

When Herod the Great died, his kingdom was partitioned and his eldest son, Archelaus, inherited Judea, Samaria and Idumea, but serious misgovernment led to his banishment. His brother, Antipas, ruled Galilee and Perea; the fact that this area rapidly became a refuge for patriots and agitators against Rome suggests that its ruler would not have been a threat to the life of the child Jesus. We can imagine, maybe, that, as a carpenter, Joseph settled in Nazareth because he could find employment in the neighbouring city of Sepphoris, which Antipas was building as his capital.

The second part of verse 23 poses a problem as there is no exact corresponding Old Testament reference. Commentaries offer a number of possible solutions. The one I find most interesting is that 'Nazorean' is a form of the Hebrew word *nazir*, meaning 'a consecrated person'. In Numbers 6:1–21, we find the conditions for being a *nazir* and, in Judges 13—16, we find the story of a lifelong *nazir*—Samson, a heroic saviour figure. If Matthew intended this meaning, it would be a way of saying that Jesus was strong to save his people.

It is interesting to note that, in his first two chapters, Matthew has introduced Jesus in several ways: son of Abraham and David in the genealogy, Son of God and Emmanuel (1:2–25), a new Moses (2:13–15), linked with Jeremiah (vv. 16–18) and, here, possibly, a new Samson. Clearly, Matthew is keen to portray him as the all-round saviour figure, encompassing the virtues of several heroic leaders of Israelite history.

Reflection

These opening chapters of Matthew's Gospel foreshadow one of the characteristics of the new kingdom inaugurated by the birth of Jesus—that in apparent weakness, God's strength is hidden and his plan is at work.

ANDREW JONES

137

Grateful parents, glory to all people

Simeon took [Jesus] in his arms and praised God, saying, 'Master, now you are dismissing your servant in peace, according to your word; for my eyes have seen your salvation, which you have prepared in the presence of all peoples, a light for revelation to the Gentiles and for glory to your people Israel.'

These verses come in the middle of Luke's closing section of the birth story. The section (2:21–40) is divided into three: verses 21–24 and 25–38 relate the dual witness of Simeon and Anna, and then comes the concluding section, consisting of verses 39–40.

Luke draws inspiration from 1 Samuel 1—2, where Elkanah and his barren wife, Hannah, have a son, Samuel, who is presented to the Lord at the sanctuary in Shiloh. The centrepiece of the whole story, however, is what we have come to know as the 'Nunc dimittis'—the song of Simeon. Simeon, who has been waiting for 'the consolation of Israel' (Luke 2:25), can now die a happy man because he believes that, in Jesus, he has seen the Messiah.

On one level, the coming of the Messiah is a tremendous fulfilment of the promises and dreams of consolation and the start of a new reign of peace, but Simeon's song is not quite the reassurance the people were expecting. He foresees a different fate for Israel and probably, by implication, all God's people. For him, there is the 'valley of the shadow of death' ahead, not paradise. The ultimate end will be glorious, but the path towards that glory is going to be difficult. Simeon sees doom in this baby—and quite possibly the cross. Yes, Simeon sings of light and glory, but also of suffering.

As we come to the end of this series of reflections, we can note that, despite Simeon's disturbing prophecy, it contains a deep call to faith. Yes, the Messiah has been born; yes, a new age has dawned; yes, God is now fully reconciled to his people—divinity and humanity are united. The challenge is to believe all of this even in the midst of injustice and suffering.

Reflection

Faith and reality go together: faith sustains and reality informs.

ANDREW JONES

Supporting Barnabas in Schools with a gift in your will

Barnabas in Schools

For many charities, income from legacies is crucial in enabling them to plan ahead, and often provides the funding to develop new projects. Legacies make a significant difference to the ability of charities to achieve their purpose. In just this way, a legacy to support BRF's work would make a huge difference.

Take our Barnabas in Schools ministry, for example. In our increasingly secular society, fewer and fewer children are growing up with any real knowledge or understanding of the Bible or the Christian faith. We're passionate about enabling children and their teachers in primary schools to explore Christianity and the Bible creatively.

Our Barnabas RE Days, using storytelling, mime and drama, are in great demand. They explore big themes (such as 'What price peace?' looking at World War I and 'Why Narnia?' exploring 'The Chronicles of Narnia' in relation to Christianity), along with the major Christian festivals. We also offer specialist In-Service Training (INSET) sessions for teachers, along with a wide range of print and online resources. We are working with over 45,000 children each year through our schools work. In addition, we are actively contributing to the national debate about the value and place of RE in our schools and championing the vital importance of seeing RE (in particular, the teaching of Christianity) taken seriously in primary schools.

Throughout its history, BRF's ministry has been enabled thanks to the generosity of those who have shared its vision and supported its work, both by giving during their lifetime and also through legacy gifts.

A legacy gift would help fund the development and sustainability of BRF's Barnabas in Schools programme into the future. We hope you may consider a legacy gift to help us continue to take this work forward in the decades to come.

For further information about making a gift to BRF in your will or to discuss how a specific bequest could be used to develop our ministry, please contact Sophie Aldred (Head of Fundraising) or Richard Fisher (Chief Executive) by email at fundraising@brf.org. uk or by phone on 01865 319700.

This page is intentionally left blank.

The BRF
Magazine

The Gift of Years

Debbie Thrower

'Journey' is a deeply meaningful concept, especially when we think about growing older. BRF exists to resource your spiritual journey, and The Gift of Years is 'resourcing the spiritual journey of older people' in particular. Championing the fact that older people matter, we are celebrating the contribution that people make in their later years and resourcing ministry among this age group to help more people make the most of the gifts that come with increased longevity.

At the same time, there are huge challenges facing our rapidly ageing population. There is no underestimating the difficulties that longer life expectancy brings. Having a spiritual perspective on life can ease the path for those negotiating a way through longer life and inevitable physical decline, which is why the concept of 'journey' is such a significant one.

Christians believe that we all come from, and are journeying home to, the God who remembers us—literally 're-members' us. Memories of what has happened to us on our own journeys are selective. They contribute to our sense of identity. One of the tasks of old age is to sift our memories. Aberdeen University's Professor of Practical Theology, John Swinton, has said, 'Without the ability to forget, our memories cease to be uniquely important… Human memory is inevitably flawed, and open to deception and distortion. This, combined with our inherent fallenness, means that there is a real sense in which we can never know who we really are.' But, he adds, 'God is not uncertain about who we are.'

The premise that we are made in the image of God and are 'the apple of his eye' (Psalm 17:8) at *every* stage of our life underpins a Christian view of ageing. References to old age and its blessings appear throughout the Bible. Some of its greatest heroes were serving God's purposes well into old age—Abraham, Sarah, Moses and Anna, to name but a few.

A form of chaplaincy named after Anna lies at the heart of The Gift of Years. Anna appears, with Simeon, in Luke's Gospel. At the age of 84 she seized the opportunity to speak of redemption and is a fine role model of a faithful older person steeped in prayer.

Anna Chaplaincy is ecumenical, community-based and open to men and women, lay or ordained. Just as Messy Church began in a church in

Hampshire, so Anna Chaplaincy has grown out of pioneering ministry in another Hampshire town, Alton. More people are exploring this way of drawing alongside older people, helping individuals to negotiate the choppy waters of growing older in the 21st century.

Why is the journey tougher today than it might have been for previous generations? Medical advances make it possible for more of us to live longer, but the debate rages over the quality of life that such benefits afford. Families are more fragmented, many adults no longer living close to parents and grandparents. Relatives might even live on different continents and keep in touch by phone or computer. Society places a greater emphasis on being youthful, beautiful and productive. When older people are no longer economically active and health concerns loom large for them, they can be left fearful of 'becoming a burden'.

The message that older people matter is deeply countercultural. Churches dare not overlook the spiritual (as well as practical) needs of men and women in their later years—the widows, widowers those who are frail and dying—for younger generations are looking at the future, wondering whether the business of getting old is worth the candle.

Time spent as an Anna Chaplain convinces me of the necessity to hear the voices of older people, to share their wisdom and to see good role models of people living faithful lives, trusting in the God who made them and has cared for them along the way. It is a Christian duty to break the cycle of the fear of ageing and instil confidence instead.

While I was co-leading a course on 'Living Deeply and Well in Later Life', a day of sunshine and showers resulted in a spectacular rainbow above Lee Abbey in Devon. Many rushed outside to photograph it. One gentleman limped out rather more slowly to take in the view. He came and stood beside me, saying, 'I've come this week because my knees aren't working so well nowadays, and I need to draw more on my inner resources. Thank you for all that you're giving us.'

Such people show that wisdom comes in many guises, and some are older man- and woman-shaped! Paul said, 'We have this treasure in clay jars' (2 Corinthians 4:7). Yes, we are fragile, mortal vessels, but what an adventure it is to regard life as a journey of faith! The sixth-century Christian philosopher Boethius put it beautifully:

To see Thee is the end and the beginning;
Thou carriest me and thou goest before:
Thou art the journey and the journey's end.

Debbie Thrower is Team Leader of The Gift of Years (www.thegiftofyears.org .uk). The Gift of Years: Bible reflections for older people is now available: see page 155 to order.

A farewell and a welcome!

Karen Laister

There are always mixed feelings when one chapter comes to an end and a new one begins. I don't know if you have ever been so absorbed in a book that you didn't want it to finish. You became involved in the plot; the author had you gripped; you identified yourself with the characters, and then you reached the last page...

Editing Bible reading notes is an enormous privilege, not least because there is a special relationship between the editor, writer and reader. It is therefore sad that we are saying farewell to Naomi Starkey in this issue of *New Daylight*. However, we are really pleased that Naomi will be continuing to write for *New Daylight* after a short break of a couple of issues.

The role of a Bible reading notes editor is to nurture, explain the relevance of the Bible for everyday life and encourage Christian discipleship, helping the reader to develop a faith that is formed around the Bible and its teaching. *New Daylight* combines commentary with a devotional approach to exploring the Bible's teachings and its core themes. It is about study but it also draws on the insights and knowledge of the writer. So often, *New Daylight* speaks into our experience of life—the joys, the times of utter desolation, the times when we need to be challenged to live out our Christian faith more fully, and much more.

Putting together a team of writers that combines a good balance of content, biblical teaching, encouragement and challenge in each issue is a skill. Over the past 14 years, Naomi has commissioned writers who bring together their study and love of the Bible with their experience and reflection on Christian faith and practice. Many readers appreciate that these contributors are drawn from a wide diversity of Christian traditions and experience, providing different perspectives on the biblical text. We also ensure that we have a balance between Old and New Testament readings.

Naomi continues in her Commissioning Editor role with BRF and we are pleased that she will be writing for *New Daylight* in future issues. We also hope that she will be able to devote more time to other writing projects, following the success of *Pilgrims in the Manager*, *Good Enough Mother* and her most recent publication, *The Recovery of Love*. In January we shall be publishing *The Recovery of Hope*, a collection of her notes, celebrating her contribution to *New Daylight* during the past 14 years.

Over the past few years, Naomi has also led Quiet Days, and these have been an important aspect of her ministry at BRF. Some of you will also know that alongside her role for BRF, Naomi was ordained a deacon in the Church of Wales in 2014. When Naomi began exploring her vocation to the priesthood, it was unclear what shape this would ultimately take, but it is absolutely clear that her ministerial training, ordination and her work as a priest have influenced her writing, editing and commissioning for BRF.

New Daylight has only had three editors since it was launched in 1989. It was Shelagh Brown who had the vision for a new series for Bible reading notes. Following Shelagh's untimely death in 1997, David Winter stepped into the role for four years before Naomi became editor in 2001.

We are now very pleased to welcome Sally Welch as the new editor of *New Daylight*. Sally brings a wealth of experience to *New Daylight* as an ordained priest in the Church of England, with a number of years' experience in parish ministry. Sally currently combines a part-time Associate Minister role with being the Oxford Diocesan Spirituality Advisor.

Sally is already a BRF author and her publications include the popular *Edible Bible Crafts* and *Celebrating Festivals*. Currently in development is *Outdoor Church*, an intergenerational resource for church congregations who want practical ideas for exploring faith through outdoor activities, experiencing God through creation and nature.

In addition, Sally has written a number of books for other publishers that explore prayer and spirituality. Her particular interest is in pilgrimage and she teaches the labyrinth method of praying to create a space to find stillness and journey in our life with God. Sally has also led a BRF Quiet Day, and we hope that she will lead more in the future, providing an opportunity for *New Daylight* readers to meet her.

A new chapter signifies a change or a new direction to a story, although the structure and core elements remain the same. We are grateful to Naomi for nurturing *New Daylight* to this stage in the journey. We look forward to Sally taking *New Daylight* forward to the next stage. As the story develops, we hope and pray that *New Daylight* will continue to resource those who use it regularly to grow their discipleship, faith and understanding of God.

Karen Laister is Deputy Chief Executive of BRF.

An extract from
Comings and Goings

Comings and **Goings**

Retracing the Christmas story
through place and time

Gordon Giles

In BRF's 2015 Advent book, Gordon Giles invites us on a journey from the end of time to the beginning. Working backwards from the Advent 'Four Last Things'—death, judgement, heaven and hell—we travel via Jesus' life, death and resurrection to the events of Christmas and, finally, to the dawn of creation. En route, we visit some of the Holy Land sites associated with Gospel events. This extract is entitled 'Holding the light: Simeon and Anna', based on Luke 2:22–32, 36–38.

It is usually possible for tourists and pilgrims to visit Temple Mount (Haram al-Sharif) in Jerusalem. Muslims should go up there, Jews must not and Christians may do so, for on a raised area above the former Western Wall of the temple is situated the al-Aqsa Mosque and the Dome of the Rock. The first king of Jordan, Abdullah I, was murdered there and his tomb is nearby. The Dome of the Rock is revered by Muslims as the place from which the prophet Mohammed ascended into heaven, and also by Jews, Christians and Muslims as the place where Isaac was so nearly sacrified by Abraham (Genesis 22:1–18). Jews may not go up there because, since the temple was destroyed by the Romans after the uprising in AD70, no one can be sure exactly where the Holy of Holies was, and it is not acceptable to trangress its sacred boundaries accidentally. Only priests such as Zechariah were allowed to enter it, and then only once in their lifetime.

For Christians, it is an eerie yet beautiful place of tranquillity above the hustle and bustle of modern Jerusalem. Despite the security checks, stacked-up riot shields and machine gun-toting guards who nonchalantly stroll around, one can hope for a peaceful visit while being struck by the proximity of violence and danger. When Ariel Sharon visited the site on 28 September 2000, the Palestinians were furious and a major uprising was ignited. Sharon was elected Israeli Prime Minister within six months. He died in 2014.

The temple complex was the holiest site in Judaism, and it was customary for a firstborn male child to be taken to the temple to be redeemed (bought back) from the Lord. The custom derived from the aftermath of the Israelities' flight from Egypt under Moses: in Exodus 13:2 and 11–16 the people are told to dedicate their firstborn sons to God. There was also a sseparate tradition of the purification of the mother, 40 days after a male birth or 80 days after a female birth (Leviticus 12:6–8). It is with this rite of purification that the sacrificial turtle doves are associated: parents were expected to offer a ram and a pigeon, or, if they could not afford a ram, two doves.

Because a mother would not be able to visit the temple within the first 40 days, the two rites were often combined, such that the story in Luke can be a little confusing: Jesus is redeemed and his mother is purified at the same time. We know from the story that Mary and Joseph were devout but poor parents, keen to do the right thing by God and by their unusually conceived firstborn son. Nowadays we commemorate this event in the church year as the final day of the 40-day Christmas season—2 February, also known as Candlemas. Simeon was the first to recognise Jesus as the 'light of the Gentiles'—the saviour of all nations, not only the Jews. It is a crucial event, and is prophetic in its scope as the aged Simeon and Anna recognise and reveal who Jesus is.

There is another, fundamentally human dimension to this story, which any grandparent will recognise. Simeon and Anna were not Jesus' grandparents, of course—they were perhaps more like his godparents—but, as each of them holds the 40-day old Christ in their arms, there are resonances for anyone who holds a baby for the first time. There is something wonderfully profound, something inherently hopeful, as one generation embraces another. In their hopeful embrace of Christly youth, Simeon and Anna show us what we should hope for and embrace. They teach us to relish the salvation we have now seen through their eyes. Whatever age we are, whether we have recently turned 20, 40, 50, 60, 70 or 80, we, like Simeon and Anna, have seen the salvation that has been prepared for us in the birth, death and resurrection of Jesus Christ.

But borne upon the throne
Of Mary's gentle breast,
Watched by her duteous love,
In her fond arms at rest;
Thus to his Father's house
He comes, the heavenly guest.

There Joseph at her side
In reverent wonder stands;
And, filled with holy joy,
Old Simeon in his hands
Takes up the promised Child,
The glory of all lands.

JOHN ELLERTON (1826–93)

The Revd Dr Gordon Giles is Vicar of St Mary Magdalene's Church in Enfield, North London and has led many pilgrimages to the Holy Land.

Recommended reading

Kevin Ball

Who wrote Mark's Gospel? At first glance, this may seem a ridiculous question and not one you've thought much about. Mark's name isn't on the list of the twelve disciples, yet, remarkably, large chunks of his Gospel appear in both Matthew and Luke's Gospels, suggesting that his writing was highly respected from the earliest times of the church. So how did this come about?

Jeremy Duff provides insightful answers in his new book *Peter's Preaching: The message of Mark's Gospel*, revealing that an ancient source describes Mark as Peter's translator to a Greek-speaking world. Intriguingly, the same source tells us that, while Mark recorded Peter's stories of Jesus 'accurately', he did not record them 'in order'. Mark devised his own sequence for the stories, for his own purpose, using a structure and format as radical in the first century as ebooks are today.

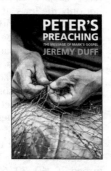

That is only the start of Jeremy's detective work in this stimulating book, which tries to uncover Peter's thought process on the key themes of the Christian message. Jeremy pieces them together like a jigsaw to reveal the full picture of Peter's understanding and explains and how that understanding helps us to grasp the radical nature of the Christian faith in those early years of the church.

So why didn't Mark present Peter's preaching in this same way? What was his purpose in presenting Peter's account 'out of order'? Jeremy turns his attention to this in the second part of the book, noting, as many previous commentators have done, that the key is the 'hinge' in the middle of the Gospel, with Peter's 'confession of faith' on the road to Caesarea Philippi and the transfiguration (Mark 8:27—9:8). Up to this point, Mark uses Peter's stories to explore the question 'Who is Jesus?' At the hinge point, Peter gives the right answer, 'You are the

Messiah', which serves only to open up a deeper question: what does that mean? The second part of the Gospel explores this question in the extended details of the events leading to the crucifixion.

The work done by Jeremy to uncover Peter's preaching illuminates Mark's purpose, which can only be found in understanding Jesus' radical way of approaching life and relationships. Unlike so many leaders of our time, Jesus embodies his radical message: the message and the person cannot be separated. There are no inconsistencies shaped by a need to appeal to prevailing cultural moods; there is no hiding behind carefully selected statistics presented as soundbites; there is nothing to expose in a scandal. Mark's challenge to his readers was and always will be: 'From my stories, who do you think Jesus is and are you ready to embrace his countercultural revolution?

Peter's Preaching
The message of Mark's Gospel
Jeremy Duff
pb, 978 0 85746 350 0, £9.99. Also available for Kindle

What is contemplation? Perhaps this is another question that you have not often considered. Contemplation is an approach to spiritual living that has a very long history. It has helped many people to plumb the depths of prayer, through silence, to hear God's voice and discover a relationship with him not experienced previously.

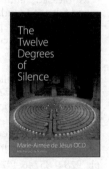

Much of the discussion on the theme from past centuries appears in the writings of the so-called Christian mystics, whose work was propelled by love and the desire for inner perfection. The mystics detail the course of this interior scrutiny and document their journey with imagery to help define the way. For instance, St Teresa of Avila used the rooms of a castle; St Clare of Assisi, a mirror; St Catherine of Siena, a bridge; and St Thérèse of Lisieux, a flower.

Nineteenth-century French Carmelite nun Sister Marie-Aimée de Jésus introduces another way, progressing by degrees to explore the channel to God that is provided through silence—a way that Carmelite writer Edith Stein has brought to wider attention. Sister Marie-Aimée's work is edited and translated into English by Lucinda M. Vardey in *The Twelve Degrees of Silence*.

Much of Marie-Aimée's spirituality and approach to exploring the interior self before God was influenced by the writings of St John of the Cross. What differentiates John's and Marie-Aimée's contributions, however, is that his work defines the rule, while hers provides directions. *The Twelve Degrees of Silence*, through probing questions for reflection, points to the stages a person needs to undergo to bring 'Jesus to life' within and to be transformed slowly to the place where 'there will be nothing left but Christ'.

There is no formal methodology for praying the twelve degrees, but the degrees themselves, by their very nature, fall into four specific groups.

- Marie-Aimée regards the first three degrees as preparation to becoming 'the silent servant of Divine Love'. They cover Silence in Words, Silence in Actions and Silence with One's Imagination.
- The next three open us up to hear 'the first note of the sacred song, the song of the heavens': Silence with One's Memories, Silence with Others and Silence with One's Heart.
- The following three are aids to perfecting a simple purity, considered as 'blessed childhood': Silence to Self-Interest, Silence of the Mind and Silence to Judgements.
- The last three prepare and experience the gift of silence as an eternal state of unity: Silence to the Will, Silence towards Oneself and Silence with God.

Whatever happens, the assurance that all will certainly be better than it was, that the rewards and treasures are indeed worth the toil, is what draws us to journey. (Sister Marie-Aimée de Jésus)

The Twelve Degrees of Silence
Marie-Aimée de Jésus OCD
pb, 978 0 85746 407 1, 80 pages, £6.99

You can look inside and find out more about all BRF books on our website: www.brfonline.org. You can also follow us on Twitter: @brfonline and like us on Facebook, www.facebook.com/biblereadingfellowship.

As a Christian charity, BRF is involved in seven complementary areas.

- **BRF** (www.brf.org.uk) resources adults for their spiritual journey through Bible reading notes, books and Quiet Days. BRF also provides the infrastructure that supports our other specialist ministries.
- **Messy Church** (www.messychurch.org.uk), led by Lucy Moore, enables churches all over the UK (and increasingly abroad) to reach children and adults beyond the fringes of the church.
- **Barnabas in Churches** (www.barnabasinchurches.org.uk) helps churches to support, resource and develop their children's ministry with the under-11s more effectively .
- **Barnabas in Schools** (www.barnabasinschools.org.uk) enables primary school children and teachers to explore Christianity creatively and bring the Bible alive within RE and Collective Worship.
- **Faith in Homes** (www.faithinhomes.org.uk) supports families to explore and live out the Christian faith at home.
- **Who Let The Dads Out** (www.wholetthedadsout.org) inspires churches to engage with dads and their pre-school children.
- **The Gift of Years** (www.brf.org.uk/thegiftofyears) celebrates the blessings of long life and seeks to meet the spiritual needs of older people.

At the heart of BRF's ministry is a desire to equip adults and children for Christian living—helping them to read and understand the Bible, explore prayer and grow as disciples of Jesus. We need your help to make an impact on the local church, local schools and the wider community.

- You could support BRF's ministry with a one-off gift or regular donation (using the response form on page 153).
- You could consider making a bequest to BRF in your will.
- You could encourage your church to support BRF as part of your church's giving to home mission—perhaps focusing on a specific area of our ministry, or a particular member of our Barnabas team.
- Most important of all, you could support BRF with your prayers.

If you would like to discuss how a specific gift or bequest could be used in the development of our ministry, please phone 01865 319700 or email enquiries@brf.org.uk.

Whatever you can do or give, we thank you for your support.

BRF has been helping individuals connect with the Bible for over 90 years. We want to support churches as they seek to encourage church members into regular Bible reading.

Order a Bible reading resources pack

This pack is designed to give your church the tools to publicise our Bible reading notes. It includes:

- Sample Bible reading notes for your congregation to try.
- Publicity resources, including a poster.
- A church magazine feature about Bible reading notes.

The pack is free, but we welcome a £5 donation to cover the cost of postage. If you require a pack to be sent outside the UK or require a specific number of sample Bible reading notes, please contact us for postage costs. More information about what the current pack contains is available on our website.

How to order and find out more

- Visit www.biblereadingnotes.org.uk/for-churches/
- Telephone BRF on 01865 319700 between 9.15 am and 5.30 pm.
- Write to us at BRF, 15 The Chambers, Vineyard, Abingdon, OX14 3FE

Keep informed about our latest initiatives

We are continuing to develop resources to help churches encourage people into regular Bible reading, wherever they are on their journey. Join our email list at www.biblereadingnotes.org.uk/helpingchurches/ to stay informed about the latest initiatives that your church could benefit from.

Introduce a friend to our notes

We can send information about our notes and current prices for you to pass on. Please contact us.

BRF MINISTRY APPEAL RESPONSE FORM

I would like to help BRF. Please use my gift for:

❏ Where most needed ❏ Barnabas Children's Ministry ❏ Messy Church
❏ Who Let The Dads Out? ❏ The Gift of Years

Please complete all relevant sections of this form and print clearly.

Title _____ First name/initials _____ Surname _____
Address _____
_____ Postcode _____
Telephone _____ Email _____

Regular giving

If you would like to give by direct debit, please tick the box below and fill in details:

❏ I would like to make a regular gift of £ _____ per month / quarter / year
(delete as appropriate) by Direct Debit. (Please complete the form on page 159.)

If you would like to give by standing order, please contact Priscilla Kew (tel: 01235 462305; email priscilla.kew@brf.org.uk; write to BRF address below).

One-off donation

Please accept my special gift of
❏ £10 ❏ £50 ❏ £100 (other) £ _____ by

❏ Cheque / Charity Voucher payable to 'BRF'
❏ Visa / Mastercard / Charity Card
(delete as appropriate)

Name on card _____

Card no. ⬚⬚⬚⬚ ⬚⬚⬚⬚ ⬚⬚⬚⬚ ⬚⬚⬚⬚

Start date ⬚⬚ ⬚⬚   Expiry date ⬚⬚ ⬚⬚

Security code ⬚⬚⬚

Signature _____ Date _____

❏ I would like to give a legacy to BRF. Please send me further information.

❏ I want BRF to claim back tax on this gift.
(If you tick this box, please fill in gift aid declaration overleaf.)

Please detach and send this completed form to: BRF, 15 The Chambers, Vineyard, Abingdon OX14 3FE.   BRF is a Registered Charity (No.233280)

GIFT AID DECLARATION

Bible Reading Fellowship

Please treat as Gift Aid donations all qualifying gifts of money made:

today ☐   in the past 4 years ☐   in the future ☐

I confirm I have paid or will pay an amount of Income Tax and/or Capital Gains Tax for each tax year (6 April to 5 April) that is at least equal to the amount of tax that all the charities that I donate to will reclaim on my gifts for that tax year. I understand that other taxes such as VAT or Council Tax do not qualify. I understand that BRF will reclaim 25p of tax on every £1 that I give.

☐   My donation does not qualify for Gift Aid.

Signature _____

Date _____

Notes:

1. Please notify BRF if you want to cancel this declaration, change your name or home address, or no longer pay sufficient tax on your income and/or capital gains.

2. If you pay Income Tax at the higher/additional rate and want to receive the additional tax relief due to you, you must include all your Gift Aid donations on your Self-Assessment tax return or ask HM Revenue and Customs to adjust your tax code.

BRF PUBLICATIONS ORDER FORM

Please send me the following book(s):

		Quantity	Price	Total
376 0	Comings and Goings (G. Giles)	_____	£7.99	_____
350 0	Peter's Preaching (J. Duff)	_____	£9.99	_____
407 1	The Twelve Degrees of Silence (Marie-Aimée de Jésus)	_____	£5.99	_____
424 8	The Word Was God (A. John)	_____	£6.99	_____
651 1	Mary (A. Jones)	_____	£8.99	_____
353 1	The Barnabas 365 Story Bible (S.A. Wright)	_____	£12.99	_____
178 0	My Keepsake Bible (S.A. Wright)	_____	£8.99	_____
412 5	The Barnabas Page-a-Day Bible (R. Davies)	_____	£10.99	_____
380 7	The Whoosh Bible (G. Robins)	_____	£12.99	_____
413 2	The Gift of Years (Bible reading notes)	_____	£2.50	_____

POSTAGE AND PACKING CHARGES				
Order value	UK	Europe	Economy (Surface)	Standard (Air)
Under £7.00	£1.25	£3.00	£3.50	£5.50
£7.00–£29.00	£2.25	£5.50	£6.50	£10.00
£30.00 & over	free	prices on request		

Total for books £ _____
Donation £ _____
Post & packing £ _____
TOTAL £ _____

Please complete the payment details below and send with payment to: **BRF, 15 The Chambers, Vineyard, Abingdon OX14 3FE**

Name _____

Address _____

_____ Postcode _____

Tel _____ Email _____

Total enclosed £ _____ (cheques should be made payable to 'BRF')

Please charge my Visa ❑ Mastercard ❑ Switch card ❑ with £ _____

Card no: ⬜⬜⬜⬜ ⬜⬜⬜⬜ ⬜⬜⬜⬜ ⬜⬜⬜⬜ ⬜⬜⬜⬜

Expires ⬜⬜⬜⬜ Security code ⬜⬜⬜

Issue no (Switch only) ⬜⬜⬜⬜

Signature (essential if paying by credit/Switch) _____

NEW DAYLIGHT INDIVIDUAL SUBSCRIPTIONS

❑ I would like to take out a subscription myself:

Your name _____

Your address _____

_____ Postcode _____

Tel _____ Email _____

Please send *New Daylight* beginning with the January 2016 / May 2016 / September 2016 issue: (delete as applicable)

(please tick box)	UK	Europe/Economy	Standard
NEW DAYLIGHT	❑ £16.35	❑ £24.00	❑ £27.60
NEW DAYLIGHT 3-year sub	❑ £42.75		
NEW DAYLIGHT DELUXE	❑ £20.70	❑ £32.70	❑ £37.95
NEW DAYLIGHT daily email only	❑ £12.90 (UK and overseas)		

Please complete the payment details below and send with appropriate payment to: **BRF, 15 The Chambers, Vineyard, Abingdon OX14 3FE**

Total enclosed £ _____ (cheques should be made payable to 'BRF')

Please charge my Visa ❑ Mastercard ❑ Switch card ❑ with £ _____

Card no: ☐☐☐☐ ☐☐☐☐ ☐☐☐☐ ☐☐☐☐ ☐☐☐☐

Expires ☐☐☐☐ Security code ☐☐☐

Issue no (Switch only) ☐☐☐☐

Signature (essential if paying by card) _____

To set up a direct debit, please also complete the form on page 159 and send it to BRF with this form.

BRF is a Registered Charity

ND0315

❏ I would like to give a gift subscription (please provide both names and addresses:

Your name _____

Your address _____

_____ Postcode _____

Tel _____ Email _____

Gift subscription name _____
Gift subscription address _____

_____ Postcode _____

Gift message (20 words max. or include your own gift card for the recipient)

_____

_____

Please send *New Daylight* beginning with the January 2016 / May 2016 / September 2016 issue: (delete as applicable)

(please tick box)	UK	Europe/Economy	Standard
NEW DAYLIGHT	❏ £16.35	❏ £24.00	❏ £27.60
NEW DAYLIGHT 3-year sub	❏ £42.75		
NEW DAYLIGHT DELUXE	❏ £20.70	❏ £32.70	❏ £37.95
NEW DAYLIGHT daily email only	❏ £12.90 (UK and overseas)		

Please complete the payment details below and send with appropriate payment to: **BRF, 15 The Chambers, Vineyard, Abingdon OX14 3FE**

Total enclosed £ _____ (cheques should be made payable to 'BRF')

Please charge my Visa ❏ Mastercard ❏ Switch card ❏ with £ _____

Card no: ⬚⬚⬚⬚⬚⬚⬚⬚⬚⬚⬚⬚⬚⬚⬚⬚⬚⬚⬚⬚

Expires ⬚⬚⬚⬚ Security code ⬚⬚⬚

Issue no (Switch only) ⬚⬚⬚⬚

Signature (essential if paying by card) _____

To set up a direct debit, please also complete the form on page 159 and send it to BRF with this form.

DIRECT DEBIT PAYMENTS

Now you can pay for your annual subscription to BRF notes using Direct Debit. You need only give your bank details once, and the payment is made automatically every year until you cancel it. If you would like to pay by Direct Debit, please use the form opposite, entering your BRF account number under 'Reference'.

You are fully covered by the Direct Debit Guarantee:

The Direct Debit Guarantee

- This Guarantee is offered by all banks and building societies that accept instructions to pay Direct Debits.
- If there are any changes to the amount, date or frequency of your Direct Debit, The Bible Reading Fellowship will notify you 10 working days in advance of your account being debited or as otherwise agreed. If you request The Bible Reading Fellowship to collect a payment, confirmation of the amount and date will be given to you at the time of the request.
- If an error is made in the payment of your Direct Debit, by The Bible Reading Fellowship or your bank or building society, you are entitled to a full and immediate refund of the amount paid from your bank or building society.
  - – If you receive a refund you are not entitled to, you must pay it back when The Bible Reading Fellowship asks you to.
- You can cancel a Direct Debit at any time by simply contacting your bank or building society. Written confirmation may be required. Please also notify us.

The Bible Reading Fellowship

Instruction to your bank or building society to pay by Direct Debit

Please fill in the whole form using a ballpoint pen and send to The Bible Reading Fellowship, 15 The Chambers, Vineyard, Abingdon OX14 3FE.

Service User Number: | 5 | 5 | 8 | 2 | 2 | 9 |

Name and full postal address of your bank or building society

To: The Manager	Bank/Building Society
Address	
	Postcode

Name(s) of account holder(s)

Branch sort code

Bank/Building Society account number

Reference

Instruction to your Bank/Building Society

Please pay The Bible Reading Fellowship Direct Debits from the account detailed in this instruction, subject to the safeguards assured by the Direct Debit Guarantee.
I understand that this instruction may remain with The Bible Reading Fellowship and, if so, details will be passed electronically to my bank/building society.

Signature(s)	
Date	

Banks and Building Societies may not accept Direct Debit instructions for some types of account.

This page is intentionally left blank.